A GOLDEN TREATISE OF MENTAL PRAYER

A GOLDEN TREATISE OF MENTAL PRAYER,

WITH

DIVERS SPIRITUAL RULES AND DIRECTIONS,

NO LESS PROFITABLE, THAN NECESSARY, FOR ALL SORTS OF PEOPLE.

FIRST COMPOSED BY THE VENERABLE AND BLESSED

FATHER FR. PETER DE ALCANTARA

OF THE SERAPHICAL ORDER OF ST. FRANCIS,

Beatified the 18th of April, 1622.

TRANSLATED INTO ENGLISH,

BY GILES WILLOUGHBY.

TO WHICH IS PREFIXED, A BRIEF RELATION OF THE LIFE AND DEATH OF THE SAME FATHER, WRITTEN BY GILES WILLOUGHBY, OF THE SAME ORDER AND OBSERVANCE.

ISBN: 978-93-5128-861-9(HB)

First Published in 1844
Indian Reprint in 2017

Published by

Kalpaz Publications
C-30, Satyawati Nagar,
Delhi – 110052
E-mail: kalpaz@hotmail.com
Website: kalpazpublications.com
Ph.: +91-9212142040

Cataloging in Publication Data—DK
Courtesy: D.K. Agencies (P) Ltd. <docinfo@dkagencies.com>

Peter, *of Alcantara, Saint,* 1499-1562, **author.**
[Tratado de la oracioìn y meditacioìn. English]
A golden treatise of mental prayer : with diverse spiritual rules and directions, no less profitable, than necessary, for all sorts of people, first composed by the venerable and blessed Father Fr. Peter De Alcantara of the Seraphical Order of St. Francis Beatified the 18th of April, 1622 / translated into English by Giles Willoughby, to which is prefixed a brief relation of the life and death of the same father written by Giles Willoughby, of the same order and observance.
pages cm
Translated from Spanish.
Reprint. Originally published: Liverpool : Booker and Co., 1844.
ISBN 9789351288619

1. Prayer—Christianity—Early works to 1800. 2. Meditation—Catholic Church—Early works to 1800. I. Willoughby, Giles, translator. II. Title.

BV4837.P3813 2017 DDC 242 23

BRIEF RELATION
OF
THE LIFE AND DEATH
OF
THE BLESSED FATHER,
FR. PETER DE ALCANTARA,
FRANCISCAN FRIAR,

WRITTEN BY GILES WILLOUGHBY, OF THE SAME ORDER AND OBSERVANCE.

THE PROLOGUE.

MISERICORDIAS Domini in æternum cantabo: "*I will sing the mercies of our Lord for ever,**" saith that kingly Prophet David. And not without cause; for, so great and unspeakable are the mercy-works of the Almighty, which out of the bowels of his infinite goodness, he hath shewed to mankind, from the first instant of his creation, that the tongues of men and angels are never able to express them.

How wonderful was this benefit; that creating man after his own† image and likeness,‡

* Psalm 88. † Gen. i. v. 26.
‡ Magister Sent. lib. 2. dist. 20.

he would have made him partaker of eternal felicity, and vested with his original justice, without death,* or any passage by misery, would have associated him with the company of angels, if he had not, by his own default, violated the laws of his creator. Notwithstanding this act of malice, the divine clemency would not suffer the work of his powerful hands so to perish, but he, according to the diversity of times,† always ordained opportune remedies, to reduce wandering man to the right way of his own salvation. Now manifesting his divine pleasure, by the means of angels, now sending the patriarchs replenished with his heavenly grace, who by their good example, might stir them up to piety; then sending the prophets illuminated with his holy spirit, not only to preach the present benefits exhibited to mankind, but also to foretell the future incarnation of the Son of God, with the mystery of his death and passion, by means of which, man should be loosed from the power of Satan, and eased of the heavy load of his transgressions.

* Gabriel. lib. 2. dist. 19, quæst. unica. art. 2.

† Scotus lib. 4. dist. 1. qu. 7. n. 2.

Thus far hath that impenetrable abyss of the divine clemency sweetly disposed all things, requisite for the saving of the soul of man. But if we will extend our thoughts a little further, and call to mind the great benefits, still heaped upon man, after the ascension of our Blessed Saviour, we shall find them innumerable. Who is not astonished at the vocation of mankind, that the apostolical trumpet of a few men, sounding to human ears, the evangelical truth, through the whole world, shall rouse up* souls, making them† happy, and thrice happy, to forsake all worldly vanities? to betake themselves to a state of perfection; to sell all they have and give to the poor; to live in perpetual chastity, and simple obedience, to

* (Religiosi) Ecclesiæ pars selectior, et sapientior; si quidem ii sapientiores habendi sunt, quam reliquum mortalium vulgus, qui se ipsos à mundi consortio segregarunt, ut vitam suam Deo consecrarunt Nazianz, ora in laudem Basilii.

† Beati illi certè, ac ter beati, ut qui Dei amore flagrarunt, atque ob ejus amorem omnia pro nihilo duxerunt, siquidem lacrymas profunderunt dieque ac nocte in luctu versati sunt, ut æternam consolationem adipiscerentur; carnes suas fame et siti, et vigiliis confecerunt, ut illic paradisi diliciæ, et gaudia illos exceperent. Damascen. in hist. B. Josaphat.

spend their days in rigorous penance, watching, fasting, and prayer, and finally to renounce all the seeming pleasures, for true there are none,* which the flattering world could afford unto them.

These things are daily put in practice by many, who profess the gospel of Christ. For, where Catholic religion flourisheth, we see divers monasteries of men and women, filled with religious souls, who consecrate themselves a perpetual sacrifice to the Almighty.

How many religious do we see honored with priestly function, an office requiring more than human purity,† and a burthen scarcely

* Consalatio mundi villis, et ad nihilum utilis, et quod magis metuendum est, veræ et salubris consolationis impedimentum. D. Ber. in ser. vir. Natui sic se habent universa sub sole, ut nihil sit in eis verè jucundum omnis siquidem laboris remedium, alterius laboris initium est. Idem in sermone de primordiis et mediis noviss. Vide plura apud Hieron. Platum de bono Stat. Relig. l. 3. cap. 1.

† Quo non oportet esse, puriorem tali fruentum sacrificio ? quo solari radio non splendidiorem manum carnem hanc dividentem ? Os quod igni spiritali repletur, linguam quæ tremendo nimis sanguine rubescit. Sic D. Chrys. hom. 83. in Matt. And Pope Gelasius, writing to Bishop Alpidius, doth excellently set down

to be supported by angel's shoulders, executing their charge with great integrity of mind; careful of their own, and zealous of the saving of their neighbors' souls: who, by their holy doctrine and exemplary lives, preach to the Christian world a reformation; who spare no pains or tedious travels, to propagate the faith of Jesus Christ to heathens and infidels; who courageously labor in Almighty God's vineyard, exposing their lives for the name of Jesus. Indies, both east and west, are witnesses of

the great purity required to priestly function saying, "Sacrosancta religio quæ Catholicam continet disciplinam, tantam sibi reverentiam vendicat, ut ad eam quilibet nisi pura conscientia, non audeat pervenire; nam, quomodo ad divini mysterii consecrationem cœlestis spiritus invocatus adveniat, si sacerdos et qui eam adesse deprecetur criminosis plenus actionibus reprobetur?" 1 q. 1 c. SACROSANCTA. Although a wicked priest doth consecrate and administer the sacraments truly, yet he sinneth grievously in consecrating and administering unworthily: "Sacrificia impiorum eis ipsis oberunt qui offerunt impie." 1 q. 1 c. PER ISAIAM. "Necesse est, ut esse munda studeat manus, quæ diluere sordes curat: ne tacta quæque deteriùs inquinet, si sordida ipsa stercoris lutum tenet." Greg. in regesto. l. 1. Epist. 24, et ponitur 1 q. 1 c. NECESSE EST.

their zealous and heroic spirits, there they sealed the truth of the gospel with the effusion of their sacred blood: yea, what acts memorable in the Church of God are there, wherein* these men have not had a very great stroke? And, finally, they so well employ and multiply those talents which the great Commander of heaven and earth hath bestowed upon them here, that assuredly they may expect an eternal reward in the kingdom of heaven hereafter.

But that which is more admirable to see, a multitude of the weaker sex abandon all worldly pleasures, they who in the world might have swum in bravery, and have had all things at their own command, to inclose themsclves in a retired cloister; there to spend their days in penance, and to consecrate the very flower of their springing youth a sweet-smelling sacrifice to their celestial spouse, Jesus Christ. These, truly, are those that† fill and beautify the garden of paradise with

* Hieron. Platus de bono status relig. l. 2. c. 30.

† Nuptia replent terram virginitas paradisum. D. Hieron.

lilies of purity: these are the flowers‡ of our holy mother, the Catholic Church, which make her glorious and fruitful. These are they that make that happy change, a moment's fading pleasure for an immortal crown of glory.

Thus we see perpetual rivers streaming from the fountain of Almighty God's mercy. But let us descend a little further into his abundant charity, and take notice of his Fatherly providence, that in process of declining times, when the blood of our Redeemer hath often begun to wax cold in the hearts of men, he would not suffer it altogether to be extinguished, but according to variety of times, never ceased to repair his church, by the ministry of some elected servants, whom he sent into this world as second Apostles, who by their

‡ "Flos est ille Ecclesiastici germinis, decus atque ornamentum gratiæ spiritualis, latæ, indolis, laudis et honoris, opus integrum atque incorruptum Dei imago respondens, ad sanctimoniam Domini, illustrior portio gregis Christi, gaudet per ipsas, atque in illis largiter floret S. Matris Ecclesiæ gloriosa fæcunditas, quantoque plus gloriosa Virginitas numero suo addit, tanto plus gaudium matris augescit. Cypr. de habit. virg. l. 4. c. 24.

example and doctrine, might draw men out of the mire of their sins, renew the fervor of our Blessed Saviour's passion, and reduce collapsed discipline to her former rigor. Many hath he sent for this end, and amongst many this blessed saint, St. Peter de Alcantara, a man, from his very cradle, consecrated to evangelical perfection; he was a faithful laborer in our Lord's vineyard, with great fidelity performing his commanded task, as it will plainly appear by that which followeth in his life.

THE TABLE OF CONTENTS.

THE SECOND PART.

CHAPTER I.

OF THE BIRTH AND EDUCATION OF BLESSED ALCANTARA AND OF HIS ENTERING INTO RELIGION.

THIS blessed Saint was born at Norba Cæsarea,* vulgarly called Alcantara, in the year of our Lord 1449, in the reign of Pope Alexander the Sixth, and Ferdinando, Catholic King of Spain. His father was called Bachilier Garavito, and his mother Maria Villela de Senabria, both of good quality, but especially honored for their virtues.

They brought up their young son in the fear of God, and sowed in him the seeds of virtue; they put him to school where, as he profited in learning, so his obedience towards his parents did likewise increase. Although he was a child, yet he withdrew himself from the common sports of children, and sorted himself amongst men, whom he saw inclined to devotion. In these his tender years, he addicted himself to the works of mercy: he applied himself seriously to learn the Christian doctrine; he often visited churches, and holy

* Civitas Hispaniæ militia ordinis Alcantarenis clara. Iste ordo prout constat ex priuil egio, illi concesso A. D. 1174, fuit institutus a Domino Gomesio Hernandes tempore Ferdinandi 2. Regis et approbatus ab Alex. 3. Lucio 3, and Innoc. 4. Rod. qq. Reg. to. 1. qu. 4. art. 4.

places, he frequented the sacraments, and continually employed himself in good works: all which did abundantly presage his future sanctity; but more confirmed it, by that which followed immediately, for he was scarce sixteen years of age, when, before he knew, he began to loath the world, and when the young sparks of his virtues began to break into a flame of devotion. He opened the doors of his soul to the inspirations of the Holy Ghost: and as he excelled his fellow students in science, so he knew that all *science, was ignorance without the right knowledge of God. Therefore, from that time forward he applied his mind to heavenly wisdom, and busied himself chiefly to know what should be most acceptable to his Sacred Majesty.

About that time, there was a famous and reformed monastery of Franciscans in the province of St. Gabriel, three miles from Valentia, whither he addressed himself, there to bring his good desires to a joyful period. But as he went along towards this place, he came to a great river, called Tiartar, which, without boat, was impossible to be passed over. He seeing this unexpected bar, to stop his happy journey, looked about, hoping to espy some waterman, who might carry him over, but when he could see none to give him any assist-

* Quid profuerit ea quæ agenda sunt scire ei qui ea ad opus non perducit. D. Chrys. Hom. 13, ad Rom

ance, he cast his eyes to heaven, and with great anxiety lamented this unhappy hinderance. Behold! upon the sudden (as he himself related,)* he was miraculously transported on the other side of the river, without any notable motion, that he could perceive.

This miracle was not unlike to that, when the river Jordan stood still for the children of Israel to pass; or when St. Peter walked upon the waves of the sea; and, indeed, it was no small beginning of Almighty God's many favors, exhibited to this blessed saint.

This obstacle being removed, he passed the other part of his way (the Holy Ghost being his guide) without any difficulty, and at length arrived to his desired harbor, this solitary monastery, situated amongst great rocks, which they commonly call *Los Manxeredes*, where he came to the fathers, and asked the habit of St. Francis of them, who did grant it to him with as much charity, as he begged it with humility.

But, when this blessed Saint considered his poor habitation, sequestered from the company of men, and abstracted from all worldly tumults; and when he saw himself vested in his penitential weed, we may well imagine with what meditations he spurred himself forward in Almighty God's service. He spake to his own soul these or the like words: behold,

* Marianus in ejus vita cap. 1.

thou hast now accomplished thy desire, thou art now arrived to the land of promise, and climbed up to the highest mountain* of Almighty God's favor to mortal man in this vale of misery, (that is,) the sacred state of a religious life, where, by how much more thou art sequestered from the pleasures of the flattering world, the more thou enjoyest the freedom of thy spirit. Thou art now come to the house of God, in which it is better for thee to be an abject than to dwell in the courts of princes. All occasions of offending thy Creator are now taken away, thy soul is now sure not to be defiled with the pitch of evil conversation. Thy company now are† terrestrial angels, who, though they live on earth, yet they have their conversation in heaven, all whose actions incite thee to nothing else but to aspire unto perfection. Thou findest here no snares to entangle thee into worldly vanities, no flatterers to applaud thee when thou dost offend, or any thing else to withdraw thy affection from the cross of Christ. Thy beloved spouse hath brought thee now into this holy desert, to recreate thy

* Hæc terra montuosa, et in sublimi sita quantum à deliciis sæculi vacat, tanto majores habet delicias spiritus. D. Hier, 1, 2, Epistolarum. Epist. 8, ad Eustochium.

† Quo nomine appellem nescio homines cœlestes an Angelos terrestres degentes in terris, sed conversationem habentes in cælis. D. Bernard. serm. ad fratres de monte Dei.

soul with his heavenly consolations* here abstracted from all worldly tumults, it may attend only to divine wisdom, and the noise of all temporal cares, being hushed and silent, it may be wholly employed in sacred contemplation, and ravished with eternal pleasures. Almighty God hath now wafted thee over this troublesome sea, and placed thee here, in the quiet harbor of thy salvation, in which state, in respect of thy former, thou art far more sure to† fall more seldom, rise sooner, stand more securely, live more sweetly, and die more confidently. Go to, I say, why standest thou still? why camest thou hither? Consider thy coarse habit, and see what penance it exacteth? Look upon the place, and reflect what spirit it teacheth thee? be courageous and make no delay, thy death is certain, and thy hour uncertain, the judge is at hand.‡ Alas! the pleasure of this world is short, but the punishment for it perpetual. A little suffering here and infinite glory hereafter. Thus, this new soldier

* Anima a corporeis cupiditatibus sæpius libera in aula mentis possit divinæ vacare sapientiæ, ubi omni strepitu terrenarum silente curarum, in meditationibus sanctis et in deliciis lætetur æternis, S. Leo. in ser. 8. de jejunio 10 mensis et eleem.

† In religione homo vivit purius, cadit rarius, surgit velocius, incedit cautius, quiescit securius, irroratur crebrius, purgatur citius, moritur confidentius, muneratur copiosius. Idem. Hom. simile est regnum cœlorum homini negotiatori.

‡ S. Fr. verba exhort. ad fratres.

of Christ spent his time, in holy discourses, sometimes of the majesty of Almighty God, sometimes of his own misery: although his precedent conversation to religion was a mirror of perfection, yet he stood not still in that grace he had already gotten, but continually aspired to higher, in which he far excelled his fellow novices. Two virtues were chiefly eminent in him: simplicity and purity. He likewise had a perfect oblivion of all worldly things. He greedily desired, and willingly accepted of the inferior and basest employments of the monastery. Neither did he esteem it a dishonor to him to cast himself at the feet of the friars, but was most willing to serve every one at their beck. In this his first year, he laid such grounds of humility, that in his whole life after, he was a rare example and pattern of this virtue. Neither when he was promoted to superiority, did he leave off his humble exercises. Thus going from grace to grace, from virtue to virtue, his good example was a burning lamp to give others light, to imitate his virtues, that the whole monastery began every day more and more to flourish in regular observance, and in the opinion of the world, to get a great name of sanctity.

CHAPTER II.

OF HIS NATURAL GIFTS, AND OF HIS PRUDENCE AND MORTIFICATION OF HIS EYES.

He was an elected vessel, beautified with all the jewels of virtues, and as his mind was replenished with supernatural gifts, so his body wanted not its natural graces. He was of a spare body, but comely, he had a grave and modest look, his eyes were sparkling tokens of the fire of divine love, which was in his soul invisible to the eye. There was not one member in that man which was not subordinate to the rule of reason. His speech was meek and humble, his conversation angelical. He had an excellent natural wit, joined with a happy memory: he had likewise a singular good judgment (as appeared in his government:) he was courageous in going through with business, which did tend to the honor of Almighty God, and the good of religion; he was grateful to all, giving to every one their due respect: he was dexterous in his actions, modest in correcting: and a peace-maker, reconciling those who upon any occasion, had been at jars. In his sermons he was hot, but moving: in hearing of confessions he was a helper, a counsellor, and a comforter: in his ordinary speech he was not fawning, nor biting, and his conversation without any pertinacity: and to conclude all in a few words: he was a man of another world, of whom we may justly say as* Alexander Halensis said of St. Bonaventure, that he was a man, in whom *Adam seemed not to have sinned.* He was a reformer, Prelate, Master, and pattern of perfection, of the Seraphical Order of our Holy Father St. Francis, who through so many provinces and remote kingdoms, illustrated this sacred institution; as another Apostle pre-ordained by Almighty God for this happy end.

* Antonius Possevinus in sacro apparatu de scriptoribus Eccles. tom. 1. de D. Bonavent.

CHAPTER III.

OF HIS RELIGIOUS SIMPLICITY, AND MORTIFICATION OF HIS EYES.

But to descend to particulars, wherein his religious simplicity was manifested. He was so absorbed in Almighty God, that he minded nothing of exterior things. When he was a brother, keeping the keys of the pantry, for the space of six months, there were in the pantry grapes and pomegranates, which lay so palpably, that none could choose but see them, but he, for that space, neither saw, nor smelt, much less touched them: being asked why he did not give them unto the brothers, he humbly answered, that he knew of none that were there. Another time, living four years in another cloister, he never took notice of a great tree which stood in the midst of the court, which was obvious to every one's eye. Being a year in another place, and asked what his cell was made of, he answered, he knew not whether it was of stone, or brick, or wood. And a chapel which he frequented above others, yet he knew neither situation, form, or any ornament which did belong thereunto. He was wont to say to blessed Theresa, his ghostly child, that he never knew a brother in his monastery, but only by his speech. Moreover, he was so mortified in his eyes, that wheresoever he was, he knew no difference in places, no distance of cells: and, finally, he was a dead man to all exterior things. Neither was this mortification any stupidity of nature, or want of senses, but his continual busying his thoughts upon Almighty God, a more noble, and higher object. Who could but think this chaste child of St. Francis, to have made a covenant with his eyes, not to behold a virgin? and well he might be styled that son of a dove, whose eyes were washed with the milk of innocency. He kept such a continual guard over his eyes, that he never knew any woman by her face. There was a certain noble matron famous for her virtue, who was wont, at Placentia, sometimes to visit the holy Father, for his spiritual counsel, she meeting him at Abula, saluted him, and expressed to him the difficulties of her state; he modestly denied that he ever saw the woman. If ever he opened his eyes, it was in the choir; though he had so good a memory, that he knew most part of the office without book. Being Superior, he did particularly correct this imperfection with severity: knowing nothing to be more prejudicial to the soul, than to set open those windows, at which doth enter the greater part of sin, that doth defile the heart of man.

CHAPTER IV.

WITH WHAT AUSTERITY AND MORTIFICATION THE HOLY FATHER LIVED.

Because for the most part this Holy Father lived in solitary convents, most remote from worldly tumults, or rather hermitages, all his rigorous penance could not be taken notice of by any. Nevertheless, we will set down some, which he could not hide from those with whom he conversed.

He did wear, for seven years together, a hair shirt, full of hard knots. St. Theresa affirmeth that he wore it twenty years.

Besides plates of iron, and other things wherewith he tyrannized ever his tender flesh. His disciplines were so frequent and bloody, that he seemed rather the trunk of a tree than a human body. He would never cover his head although it rained ever so fast, or the sun shined ever so hot. His diet was so slender and mean, that, in his youth, and old age, he did eat nothing but brown bread, and the most musty crusts that he could find. If sometimes he recreated himself with a few boiled herbs, he would not be so delicious as to eat them with oil. Being Superior he caused as many beans and peas to be boiled at once, as should serve the convent for seven days together, which austerity his subjects most willingly embraced, being glad, in some measure, to imitate their chief. But he seasoned his own portion with ashes, or some ungrateful liquor, lest his palate should take pleasure in his meat.

Mother Theresa hath heard his companions say, that sometimes he lived eight days together without any meat or drink, especially when with more violence, he addicted himself to devotion. For he suffered in his prayers frequent raptures and extacies, of which (saith she) I am witness. He never drank wine, but water, though, for the infirmity of his stomach, it was prescribed to him by the physician: but he constantly refused it, saying, that nothing was so repugnant to holy purity and abstinence as flesh and wine, the one being an enemy to chastity, the other to contemplation, both which, as long as he lived, by God's grace, he would enjoy. I will set down for the satisfaction of the devout reader, the words of ever blessed Theresa, the glory and foundress of the discalceated Carmelites, to whom he was sometimes ghostly father, of whom she confesseth to have received much spiritual comfort; whose authority, by reason of her renowned sanctity, and living at the same time with him, is without control. Her words be these.*

* Ex vita B. Theresæ. cap. 27.

"Almighty God bereaved us of a man of admirable example, when he took out of this life Father Peter of Alcantara. The world, it seemeth, could endure no longer so great a perfection. They say, that our health is not so good; that now those times be past, this holy man was of this time, he was fat in spirit, as those of other ages; he had also the world under his feet, for, though we do not go barefoot, nor do such austere penance as he did, there are many things (as I have said elsewhere) to tread down the world withal. And our Lord teacheth them, when he seeth such a mind, as he gave, in great measure, to this holy man, which I speak of, to continue forty-seven years together in such austere penance, as all know. I will declare some part of it, for I know that it is all true. He told it to me and to another, from whom he concealed little, and the cause why he told it me, was the great love which he bore me, and which our Lord gave him to defend me, and encourage me, in the time of so great necessity, as that was, which I have spoken of, and will declare further. It seemeth to me, that he told me, that he had slept no more than an hour and a half betwixt day and night for the space of forty years, and this was the greatest difficulty he found in his penance at the beginning, to overcome his sleep, and for this cause he did always, either kneel or stand, and when he slept it was sitting, leaning his head against a little piece of wood, which he had driven into the wall, he could not lie down, though he would, for his cell, as is known, was no longer than four feet and a half. In all these years he never put on his capuce, how great sun-shine or rain soever was; neither had he any thing on his feet, nor other garment, but his habit of coarse cloth, without any other thing next his skin, and this as straight as could be endured, and a short cloak of the same upon it. He told me that when it was very cold he did put it off, and opened the door and little window of his cell; that afterwards, when he did put his cloak on again, and shut his door, he might give some contentment and recreate his body, which before was frozen with cold. He did very ordinarily eat but once in three days; and he asked me at what I marvelled, for it was very possible for one that accustomed himself to it. His poverty was extreme, and likewise his mortification in his youth. With all his sanctity, he was very affable, though he used not many words, if he were not spoken to, for then he was very pleasing, having a good understanding. And a little after, "His end was like his life, preaching and admonishing his friars. When he saw death draw nigh, he said the psalm: "Lætatus sum in his, quæ dicta sunt mihi," and kneeling down, departed. Since our Lord hath let me enjoy him more then in his life, giving me advice and counsel in many things, I have seen him many times in exceeding great glory. The first time he appeared unto me, he said, "O happy penance which did merit such a reward!" and many other things. A year before he died, he appeared to me, being absent, and I knew that he should die, and I sent him word, being some leagues from hence. When he gave up the ghost, he appeared to me and said, that he went to rest, I believed it not, I told some of it, and eight days after the news came that he was dead, or rather began to live for ever. Behold here his austerity endeth with so great glory, he seemed to comfort me more than when he was in this world. Our Lord told me once, that nothing should be asked in his name which he would not hear. I have seen many things fulfilled, which I have desired him to ask of our Lord; he be blessed for ever. Amen." And in the thirtieth chapter of her life, she sayeth as follows: "Our Lord vouchsafed to remedy a great part of my trouble, and for that time the whole, by bringing to this place the Blessed Father Peter of Alcantara, of whom I have already made mention, and spoken something of his penance; for amongst other things, I was certified, that for twenty years he had worn a cilice of plate continually. He is the author of certain little books of prayer, which are now much used in the Spanish tongue, for as one that hath exercised it well, he wrote very profitably, giving most excellent rules to those who addicted themselves to prayer. He observed the first rule of St. Francis with all rigor, and other things which I have related before." Thus she, and so much shall suffice to speak of, but part of his rigorous penance, it was his fervent zeal, and love of God, not strength of body, which made this crabbed way of penance easy to his heroic spirit; whose example may (though not in so great a measure as he did,) justly move us to shake off that old and self-love excuse of ours, in saying, our bodies are weak, when alas! our wills are frozen, and so nice, that we are afraid to expose our body but to a poor trial. The heathen Seneca will check our indevotion, who saith:* "*Not because certain things are hard, therefore we dare not do them, but because we dare not do them, therefore they are hard.*"

* Non quia difficilia quædam sunt, ideo non audemus, sed quia non audemus, ideo difficilia.

CHAPTER V.

OF HIS GREAT PURITY AND HUMILITY.

THE man of God increasing in his rigorous penance, did not only mortify in part, but wholly subdued his passions, and made his senses subordinate to the rule of reason; he suffered nothing to enter into his soul which might separate, or in the least kind withdraw his affection from his beloved spouse, for (as much as was possible for pilgrim man,) he enjoyed the spirit of God; golden peace and divine consolation sat upon his wings of contemplation, and where others make their bodies masters, he made his a slave unto his spirit. Hence it came to pass, that many of both sex, drawn with the fragrant odour of his virtues, flocked to him, as to another Apostle, to whose counsels and admonitions they obeyed, as to a divine oracle.

Upon a time, the Count Orapsane, a devout nobleman, came to visit him, and falling into discourse, how much Almighty God was moved with the sins of the world, out of his zeal breaketh into these speeches, O Father! what do you think? what will become of this wicked world? do you think the divine justice can contain itself any longer from revenge? behold, how virtue is oppressed, and sin triumpheth? how wilfully do we hoard up anger against the day of anger? to which the man of God modestly answered and said, noble Sir, do not afflict yourself, a remedy will easily be found to cure this disease; the point of the difficulty consisteth only in you and me, for the general perdition of mankind floweth from this fountain, that all and every one dissembling or cloaking their own sins, accuse the whole, when the whole cannot be said to sin at all, but particular persons in the whole. Wherefore, men cry out against the wickedness of the world, that all are naught, and none that do good, when if they would but look into their own particular, they should find matter enough of sorrow, and to move themselves to do penance for their own faults; but now because they blame the whole, they neglect their own particulars, and justify themselves with a sottish presumption. Therefore, noble Sir, let your Lordship, and I, mend one a piece, and then a great part of the world will be amended; we shall appease the angry judge, and repair a great part of the ruin of mankind by our good example.

When Charles the Fifth recollected himself in a certain monastery of the Hieronymites, understanding of the sanctity and integrity of this holy Father, he sent for him, with an intent to make him his ghostly father. But he humbly refusing so great an honor, alleged some reasons, why he thought this employment not to be fitting for him. At which denial, the Emperor being a little moved with anger, said, we charge you, Father, that you would take care of our soul. He seeing this sudden alteration of Cæsar, fell down at the feet of his majesty, and earnestly desired him to defer the business to what day or hour he would please to appoint, that, in the mean time, he might commend it to Almighty God, which the Emperor granted; then he took his leave of the Emperor, and said, this renowned Cæsar, shall be a sign unto you, that it is not according to the will of God, which you have desired, if I do not return at the appointed time. Then passing to his former solitude, as he went, he complained with many sighs and groans to Almighty God, fearing by the devices of Satan, to be drawn from the embracings of his blessed spouse, Jesus Christ. He sent up his fervent prayers to the Almighty's throne, and said these or like words: " Lord, I have not, therefore, left the world, and betaken myself to this holy desart, that now at length my name should be renowned in a prince's court, and live in honor, that am a poor Franciscan friar. Why should my ears be troubled with flatterings of courtiers, who came to speak my fault in religion? I confess that this office may be exercised without sin; but whether it be expedient for my soul, sweet Jesus, tell me? And when he entered into his cell, Lord, I beseech thee, pull me not from hence, whither thy omnipotent hand hath brought me. Here I am safe, here I am rich; because I enjoy thee, who alone can satiate my soul. Alas! without thee what is the whole empire? and with thee, this poor cell is a kingdom of content. Here let me live: Here let me die. Lord, let it please thee what I wish for, because all is thine whatsoever I desire. If thou grantest me thy petition, let this be a sign unto me, that Cæsar molesteth me no more." So rising, as being heard, did appear no more before him. Neither did the Emperor ever solicit him after.

The same request did the illustrious Princess Joanna, sister to Philip the Second, Catholic King of Spain, make unto this holy Father, whom he likewise denied after the same manner. Thus, whilst he fled honors, he was most honored of all, and reverenced of every one.

And what candid sincerity he used in contemning proffered honors, men of no small quality observed, that those who honored him, he would no more regard their speech than a simple idiot, and would labor to divert them from that to some other discourse. He had rather be called a sinner than a holy man, and he himself would (without scandal) lay open to the world his imperfections, under which, his virtues and graces were cloaked. But God, the searcher of secrets, by how much he did strive to hide them; the more he made his fame to shine in the world, to the astonishment of all. For he was a man whom God had chosen according to his own heart, by whose industry, and from whose spiritual loins did spring many servants of Jesus Christ, and many renowned martyrs of our holy order.

CHAPTER VI.

OF HIS FERVENT PRAYERS AND RAPTURES, AND OF HIS SPIRIT OF PROPHECY.

ALMIGHTY God was always present with him, and he with God. His soul was like a fiery furnace, made hot with the fuel of the cross of Christ. It was not in his own power to contain himself, but what thing soever he either saw, or heard, which might delight his beloved Jesus, though it were but afar off, his heart-strings would begin to tremble, and his vital spirits leave him, and frequently fall into extacy. He was accustomed for a whole hour together, to say his prayers with his arms stretched out in the manner of a cross, sighing and weeping, till at last he would be beside himself, elevated from the ground, and united only to his God. He was oftentimes in this manner rapt, when he was in the choir at matins. But his devotion was much more augmented at the altar, when he celebrated the dreadful sacrifice, then would rivers of tears gush in abundance from his venerable eyes, that would move the most stony and obdurate heart of any of the standers by unto compunction. After mass he would withdraw himself into his cell, where he hath been often heard to have had grievous conflicts with devils; who oftentimes appearing in a visible shape, would follow him up and down with terrible fury.

In talking of Almighty God his soul would be presently inebriated with divine sweetness, and ascending by degrees from one word to another, as, what! was God incarnated for me? was God made man for me? was God vested with human flesh for me? and the like. He would forthwith break into exclamations, and hurrying himself into his cell, would for the space of above three hours together, lose the use of his senses.* One day, a brother that was newly made Priest, practising in the garden to sing mass, when he heard him sing these words of St. John's gospel, *(Et verbum caro factum est,)* he became enraptured, and remained for a long time in ecstacy.

This, therefore, was ordinary to the friend of God, that when he heard any thing of the humanity of our blessed Saviour, or any devout word of the holy Scripture, it would cause him raptures. Neither could he help them, though he did strive much against them, especially in the presence of others, but his heart would become like melting wax in the midst of his bowels. He was often, in seeing the crucifix, moved with such compassion, that his arms

* Marianus in vita B. Alcant. cap. 10.

would be rapt across, with little clouds glittering about his head.

He would sometimes prophesy, to some the loss of honors, to others sudden death, to others purgatory; which would fall out the very day and hour he told them.

The first time he saw St. Theresa, he told her what contradictions, and afflictions, she suffered from her ghostly fathers, and other spiritual persons, who would needs persuade her, that she was seduced; and, moreover, that she was to suffer much more in the same kind. He likewise foretold what should be the success in the *Indies*.

CHAPTER VII.

OF HIS PATIENCE.

He traced the steps of our blessed Saviour, and all his glorious saints,* all which did never merit their crowns without carrying of the cross of Christ.

He was another patient Job, in suffering the temptations, and afflictions, the infirmity of man is subject unto, he was in a particular manner loaded with the heavy burden of them, notwithstanding his fervent spirit, patiently supported, and victoriously triumphed over all his difficulties, maugre all the force of Satan. His frequent combats, his persecutions, his sickness, his long and tedious travels, the difficulties he did undergoin erecting his province, would take up too much time to relate. He was so greedy of suffering, that he esteemed himself happy, to bear afflictions for the name of Jesus, saying, that there was no way so sure and easy to attain unto perfection, as the carrying of the cross of Christ. He would, therefore, beg of Almighty God, that he might

* Quis Sanctorum sine patientia coronatus ? solus in deliciis Solomon fuit, et ideo fortase corruit. Div. Hieron.

never be without some affliction. Thus did our courageous champion trample upon his enemies. *Thou shalt walk upon the Asp and the Basilisk; and thou shalt trample under foot the Lion and the Dragon.** Whilst he vanquished all his foes, not so much by resisting, as by suffering.

* Psal. 90.

CHAPTER VIII.

OF HIS CHARITY TOWARDS HIS NEIGHBOR.

His charity towards his neighbor was unspeakable; for this cause he often visited hospitals to serve the sick, assisting them both spiritually and corporally, and oftentimes miraculously restoring them to their former health. After he had made an end of his devotion, the residue of his time he spent in comforting the afflicted, in cherishing the feeble, and, finally, in anything he could imagine might comfort his neighbor, either corporally or spiritually; so that innumerable people of all conditions and sexes, continually flocked unto him for his charitable assistance.

CHAPTER IX.

OF HIS POVERTY.

He was a rigid observer of holy poverty, which in imitation of his patron,* St. Francis, he not only loved, but honored so far that he was wont to call it the Evangelical pearl, wherewith he enriched his new province, in that lustre as the observance was in the infancy of our Seraphical Order, from which time, and by whose example, most provinces through the Christian world have excelled in this particular point, as much as in their former splendor. He permitted his brethren to have nothing in their cells of mere necessity, and to the preachers he permitted them no more than two or three books, with the Bible and a crucifix.

He was upon a time asked by St. Theresa, whether or no she should found her monasteries

* St. Franciscus non solum paupertatis commodis libentissime fruebatur, sed etiam ita honorabat et colebat, quæsirem eximiam et eni nulla humana dignitas posset comparari. Itaque ut D. Bonav. scribit, eam in omni sermone modo Matrem, modo Sponsam, modo Dominam appellabat, sæpe etiam Reginam, propterea quod in rege regum ejusque genitrice, adeo insigniter effulfisset. Hieron. Platus de bono stat. relig. lib. 2. cap. 3.

with rents and yearly revenues, to which diverse persons of quality had advised her. He answered, that it was an injury to God the author of Evangelical counsels, to ask the advice of men touching the observance of them, or to doubt whether or no they were observable. And with all encouraged her to be constant in that fervent desire, she had begun in embracing holy poverty. To whose counsel she willingly obeyed. And after, our Lord appeared to her in prayer, and declared, that it was his will that her monasteries should be founded in holy poverty. His letter to her, I think it not amiss, to set down at large, which followeth.

A LETTER

OF THE BLESSED FATHER FR. PETER DE ALCANTARA, TO THE HOLY MOTHER THERESA OF JESUS, WHO DEMANDED HIS COUNSEL, WHETHER SHE SHOULD FOUND MONASTERIES WITH RENTS OR NOT.

THE Holy Ghost give you his grace and love, &c. I received yours, delivered me by Don Gonzales d'Aranda, and am amazed considering your zeal and piety: in committing to the direction of learned lawyers, that, which is noways their profession, or belonging unto them: you should do well to take their advice concerning the deciding of a process, or of suits in law, and temporal affairs, but in that which concerns perfection of life, we ought to treat only with those who practise the same. For such as the conscience of every one is, such are his exercises and works. Concerning the Evangelical counsels, may I demand whether they be observable or no? For that the counsels of God cannot be but good, neither can the observance thereof seem difficult, unless to those who govern themselves according to human prudence, having less confidence in God than they ought. For he who hath given the counsel, will consequently give force and means to accomplish the same. And if your zeal and fervor draw you to embrace the counsels of Jesus Christ, observe them with the greatest integrity and perfection that you possibly can, seeing they were equally given to both sexes. It cannot be, but the same merit and reward will be rendered unto you, as to others that have truly observed them. And if there be seen any want or necessity in the monasteries of poor religious women, it is because they are poor against their wills, and not through fault of their vow of poverty, or following of Evangelical counsels. For I account not much of their simple poverty, but of their patient sufferance of the same for the love of God. But I more esteem that poverty which is desired, procured, and embraced for the same love. And, if I should think, or determinately believe otherwise, I should not hold myself a good Catholic. I believe in this, and in all other things taught by our blessed Saviour, and that his counsels are good and profitable, as proceeding from God, and though they oblige not to sin, they bind, nevertheless, that man to be more perfect that followeth them, than if he had not undertaken them at all. I hold them poor in spirit, who are poor in will, as our Saviour hath said, and myself proved; however, I believe more from God than of my own experience, that those, who by the grace of God are with all their hearts poor, lead a life most happy, as confiding, and hoping in him alone. His divine Majesty give you light to understand this truth, and to practise it. Believe not those that shall tell you the contrary, for want of light and understanding, or for not having tasted how sweet our Lord is to those that fear and love him, renouncing for his sake all unnecessary things of this world, for they are enemies of the cross of Christ, not believing the glory which accompanieth the same. I also pray our Lord to give you this light, that you be not wanting in the belief of this truth, so much manifested; and that you take not counsel, but of the followers of Jesus Christ; although others think it sufficient, if they observe the thing they are bound unto, yet they have not always greater virtue and perfection by their work. And though the counsel be good, yet that of our blessed Saviour is much better, who knows what he counsels, and gives grace to accomplish the same, and in the end reward to those who hope in him, and not in rents and goods of the earth.

From Avila, this 14*th day of April*, 1562.

CHAPTER X.

OF HIS CONFIDENCE IN ALMIGHTY GOD'S PROVIDENCE.

HIS admirable confidence in the providence of Almighty God accompanied his rigid and Evangelical poverty, and it oftentimes miraculously appeared both at home and abroad.

He* lived sometimes in the convent of Sancta Maria de Rosario, which is situated in a woody place, by the river Tentairis, six Italian miles remote from any company; at all times it was difficult to come to it, as the way was very steep and crooked,† nevertheless it was a place of great devotion, whither the inhabitants of the country much resorted; but now, by reason of a great snow, the like of which was not seen in the memory of man, the monastery was so environed on every side, that the friars could not go out to get their victuals, neither could any come to them to bring provision. They cried to heaven to the Father of the poor, that being destitute of all

* Marianus in ejus vita cap. 6.

† Ea est itineris ad eum ob loci solitudinem atque viarum anfractus difficultas, ut vix accolis atque assuetis pateat. Gonzaga 3 parte Chron. ord. S. Franc. in prov. Sancti Josephi.

human aid, he only, out of his infinite mercy, would be pleased not to forsake them. The holy Father desired them to go into the church, and kneeling down before the blessed Sacrament, to pray to God that he would put a remedy to their hard affliction. He with great confidence animated his brethren, saying—Be courageous, brethren, Almighty God will not be long, he will come without delay. He had no sooner uttered the words, but another most violent storm of snow fell so fast, that frustrated the hopes of all human assistance. But he that containeth not his anger long, did not delay to comfort his afflicted children. Behold! a little space after the storm was over, the porter heard the bell of the gate of the convent ring; he went to open the door, but espied nobody; he returned back again, thinking it to be the wind that had stirred the bell, or that his fancy seemed to hear the noise when he heard it not; checking himself with foolishness, that he could imagine, that it was possible for any one to come to the convent in so deep a snow. Whilst he was thus discoursing with himself, it rang again so hard that all heard it, notwithstanding there was a great wind. Then returning again to the gate, and opening it, he found a basket filled with new white bread, he looked about to see if he could espy any body, but no creature appeared, for it was a deep snow, where the footing of any person could not but appear. He left the basket, and with joy ran back into the convent, to carry the good news to the friars, who would not believe, until the holy Father commanded all the brothers to go in manner of procession, to see what Almighty God had done for his servants ;,when they came, they found all true, as the porter had related to them; but their benefactor did no where visibly appear. They arried the basket in, and after thanksgiving, refreshed themselves with the bread which the Father of heaven had miraculously bestowed upon them. Upon which they lived many days, until the extremity of the season was past, and they could go out to beg alms according to their custom.

Another time* travelling in the extremity of the heat of summer, upon the mountain vulgarly called Sierra Morena, he, with his companion, grew so faint, for want of something to quench their thirst, that they were ready to sink under the burden of their tedious journey. He said unto his companion, Brother, let us betake ourselves to prayer, the only remedy to incline the God of mercy to take compassion upon our misery. Whilst they were upon their knees at prayers, from a thicket came running out a mad bull, which made towards them amain; they seeing themselves in this great danger of their lives, betook themselves to flight, but the bull pursued them

* Marianus. Ibidem cap. 7.

over hedge and ditch, hard at their heels, till at last he forced them to a place where there was a fountain of water; when they came in sight of that, the bull, forgetting his former fury, stood still like an innocent lamb, he breathed himself awhile, and went another way. But they admiring this great miracle of the Omnipotent, that sendeth his wild beasts to teach the poor, refreshed themselves, and went on their journey with alacrity, their souls more comforted with this unexpected benefit of Almighty God's providence, than their bodies strengthened with the water which they drank for their sustenance.

Having occasion* to go from De las Lucuas to Del Pico, as he was on his journey it began to snow, which fell so fast that it was not possible for him to go forward or backward, so that he was enforced to remain the whole night in that extremity of cold and snow. But the fervor of his devotion, wherewith he implored the divine assistance, caused him to pass over the night without tediousness. But what was more admirable, behold! in the morning when it was day, one might see that the snow did not so much as touch or wet him, but it congealed over his head, in a miraculous manner, like a canopy, and on each side two walls of snow frozen in a curious manner defended him from

* Marianus. Ibidem.

the inclemency of the weather, as though he had been shut in a beautiful chamber.

These few miracles I have set down, collected out of many, which Almighty God hath been pleased to work by the means of his glorious servant, as testimonies,* not only of many singular prerogatives of graces exhibited to this holy Father in his own particular; but also, that we, admiring the strange and unaccustomed manner of Almighty God's proceedings with this blessed man, the truth whereof being confirmed by many approved authors, may be incited to imitate his virtues, whom God hath honored with the grace of working miracles.

If thou shouldst object with Calvin, *In Præfat. Instit.* that the miracles of our saints in the Catholic Church, are partly feigned, partly diabolical, I answer, that the same thing the Pharisees objected to our blessed Saviour, that he cast out devils in Beelzebub the prince of the devils. Moreover, it is most devilish to blemish the integrity of the ancient fathers and saints, with such an impudent and foul aspersion, as those who wrote the lives of other saints, as Nyssens of Thaumaturgus, St. Athanasius and St. Jerome of St. Anthony,

* Miraculum voro, quidquid arduum aut insolitum supra spem vel facultatem mirantis apparet. Quædam admirationem faciunt, quædam gratiam magnam benevolentiamque conciliant. S. August. de Util. Cred. cap. xvi.

Severus of St. Martin, St. Gregory of St. Benedict, St. Bernard of St. Malachias, St. Bonaventure of St. Francis, whose authority if we should deny, no faith or credit is to be given to any history in the world, which absurdity none but men out of their wits, or blinded with malice, will admit. St. Augustine confirmeth what I say. His words are these: "An dicet aliquis ista falsa esse miracula, nec fuisse facta, sed mendaciter scripta? Quisquis hoc dicit, si de his rebus negat omnino ullis litteris esse credendum, potest etiam dicere nec Deos ullos curare mortalia." De Civit. Dei, l. 10, c. 18.

CHAPTER XI.

OF HIS KNOWLEDGE IN HOLY SCRIPTURE, AND OF HIS PREACHING.

He was so well versed in the Holy Scripture, that for the most part, he could repeat it without book, and in explicating it, he was so clear, and withal so moving, that one might judge his learning to be rather supernaturally infused in prayer, than naturally gotten by the ordinary means of study,* for he quickly learned what he was taught, seeing he had the Holy Ghost for his master. He wrote some spiritual works, wherein he had a special gift from Almighty God, both to direct those who tend to perfection, in their journey towards heaven, as also to inflame their wills to aspire to that eternal good. In this particular science, he was chiefly eminent, and wrote profitable and learned tracts of this matter.

He had such a rare gift in preaching, such invective against sin, and withal so comfortable to those who were pulling their feet out of the snare of vices, that Almighty God was

* O quam velox est sermo sapientiæ, et ubi Deus magister est, quam cito discitur quod docetur. B. Leo ser. 1 de Pentecoste.

pleased to work by his means many wonderful effects in the souls of his auditory.

In the city of Abula there was a young gentleman who was given up to, and as it were buried in all the sports and vanities of this wicked world: but especially in the wild and pernicious love of wanton women. Coming in his pomp upon a festival day of that place, he by chance met the holy father; and, when he understood from his companions the quality and sanctity of him, he went towards him, with others, to salute him with great respect, and withal begged his prayers, but God knoweth with what intention, for he still obstinately remained in his filthy desires. But the holy father in his sermon touched the sore of his soul unto the quick, (yet not revealing any person) insomuch that the Holy Ghost did so work with him, that this prodigal child understanding the father was to go away from that place the next day, made haste to get pen and ink to write his sins, the next day cometh to the father and saluteth him, giving him a long* scroll of his sinful life, and desired him for the love of God, that he would vouchsafe to pray for him, that God would have mercy upon his soul, and that he would not punish him for ever according to his deserts. The holy father received his paper, and promised that he would pray for him.

* The young man out of humility, manifested his sins to the holy father out of the sacrament of confession.

So each departed their way. But he had scarce turned his back, but the father earnestly begged of Almighty God his conversion, of which he was presently sensible; for, before he came home, the spirit of God did so inflame him, that he abjured his former conversation, and loathed the pleasures that before he loved so much, and being returned to his house, flung off his brave clothes, tore his chain from his neck, and vested himself in mean and country clothes, without any shame of appearing to all the world, all admiring the sudden change of the right hand of the Most High; and, as afterwards, he lived well, persevering to the end, so he died happily. He dispersed his patrimony amongst the poor, and built many monasteries and hospitals, as testimonies of his conversion.

He had such efficacy in his preaching, that many common women, drawn with the sweetness of his spirit, changed their sordid and base habits of living, into holy and pious conversation. Others, as well of the nobility, as amongst the meaner sort of people, renouncing all pleasures for the love of Jesus, shrouded themselves in cloisters, where they might be secure from the contagion of worldly vanities. And many consecrating their virginity to their celestial spouse, like lilies amongst thorns, persevered in the open world amidst the dangers thereof, with immoveable constancy.

CHAPTER XII.

OF HIS RELIGIOUS ZEAL AND OF HIS DEATH.

The reverend esteem of his virtue increased so much, even in his own cloister, that there, many times (enjoined by obedience) performing the office of Guardian with great integrity, he was, at length, by the suffrages of all the fathers, elected twice Provincial of the province of St. Gabriel, where he made a happy and notable reformation. But after his three years expired, he betook himself again to his poor hermitage, where he feasted his soul with sacred contemplation, persevering in reading the ancient fathers, watchings, fastings, and regular discipline. But the more he hid himself in these obscure places, the more the fame of his learning and sanctity did shine abroad. And in testimony that Almighty God would not have this resplendent light to be put under a bushel, but to be set upon a candlestick, to give light to others to follow his glorious footsteps, and to the end that he might not only enrich his own soul with the treasures of virtue, but also instruct others, both by his doctrine and example, to aspire to heaven, the apostolic see did vouchsafe to honor him with a commission, by virtue of which, he should erect and found a new provinee, under the title of St. Joseph; which, before his death, he was so happy to see, not only multiplied in number of convents and religious men, by his great labor and travail, but also to be perfectly established in regular observance and true monastical discipline.

At last, the number of his merits being complete, his just master, whom he had served so long with great fidelity, was pleased to call him to reward his labors with an eternal crown of glory, and to reap in joy what he had sown in tears. He fell sick in the convent of St. Andrew de Monte Areno, where Almighty God vouchsafed to let him know the hour of his death: and before his departure, he called his brethren, exhorting them to perseverance in that happy course which they had undertaken for the love of God, and the saving of their own souls. He then received upon his knees, with abundance of tears, the sacred Viaticum with singular devotion, and a little after, his infirmity increasing, he received also the sacrament of Extreme Unction. The Blessed Virgin and St. John, to whom all his life he was very much devout, appeared to him, and gave him assurance of his salvation; which ever-comfortable news he no sooner understood, but his heart was ravished with joy, and his mouth filled with gladness, and out of that abundance of content he breaketh out into these words of the prophet David,* "*Lætatus sum in his quæ dicta sunt mihi : in domum Domini ibimus :*" "I have rejoiced in those things that are said unto me: we will go into the house of our Lord." In fine, the happy hour being come, he yielded his blessed soul into the hands of his maker, and by the passage of a temporal death, travelled to an eternal life, on the 18th of October, upon the feast of St. Luke, 1562, the 63d year of his age, and the 47th of his entrance into holy religion. His body after his death became more beautiful, shining with great clarity, and sending forth sweet odors. The people from all parts flocked to behold this sacred spectacle, and greedy after so rich a prey, clipped pieces of his habit, which they conserved as holy relics. His body was no sooner in the grave, but his sepulchre began to be renowned with many miracles,† which for brevity's sake I omit to speak of, because I would not be too tedious to the devout reader.

* Psalm 112.

† Cum puerulus Æthiops inutilis penitus atque contractus ad illius sepulchrum ab ejus hera uxore quondam Martini de Friars ac præfati oppidi Arrenarum accolæ, adductus esset, ejus meritis, Deo optimo maximo id operante, integræ sospitati restituitur. Et Leonora Gonsalva ejusdem oppidi inquilina a paralisi qua gravissime laborabat ad ejus quoque sepulchrum liberatur. Franc. Gonzaga, 3 parte Chron. ordinis Seraphici. Vide plura apud Joannem de Sancta Maria in vita Beati Alcant. c. 30.

His soul was no sooner out of his body,* but presently he appeared to St. Theresa, to bring unto her the joyful tidings of his reception into heaven. Many times after he appeared to her, and once, amongst the rest, he said unto her, "O happy penance that deserved such a glorious recompense."†

Happy, indeed,‡ was his penance that

* In ejus Vita, cap. 27.

† Opera nostra non habent bonitatem meritoriam gloriæ ex sua natura, nec a nobis, sed a Deo. For our works are to be taken in a twofold respect. 1. As they are in their proper nature and dignity, 2. As they have God's promise and acceptance. If we consider them in the first sense, so they do not merit salvation; if in the second they do. This I say to answer the objection of ignorant Protestants, who might take occasion to carp at this word, (deserved,) and who likewise think that we so dignify our works that thereby we think to merit heaven, abstracting from the merits of our blessed Saviour's passion, when it is certain our doctrine is, that the chief reason of merit is founded in God's promise, not man's work; and our works so to merit and to be ennobled, chiefly by virtue of their principal agent our blessed Saviour's passion.—Conradus Klingius de locis com. l. i. c. 35. Stapleton Controvers. l. x. c. 12. Bellarm. l. i. de Justificat. c. 21, et. l. v. c. 11, cum communi Doctorum.

‡ If the conversion of sinners, and of grievous sinners, be so pleasing to Almighty God, that the angels of heaven do rejoice at it, according to St. Bernard, "Denique et supernas beatorum mansiones attingit pœnitentiæ odor, ita ut, teste ipsa Veritate, magnam gaudium sit inter Angelos Dei supra uno peccatore pœnitentiam agente. Gaudete, pœnitentes; pusillanimes, confortamini. Vobis dico, quos nuper conver-

changed sorrows into pleasures, mourning into mirth, tears into joys, and a momentary cross into an eternal crown. The same blessed Theresa, as we have said before, affirmed, that she received more comfort and consolation from him after his death, than in the time of his life; and that his soul flew immediately to heaven, without any passage by purgatory. All these things being well examined, and verified by persons, without all exception, worthy of credit, his holiness, for the glory of God, honor of the saint, and benefit of the faithful, vouchsafed to pronounce him beatified, to the end that, as he had a perfect fruition of glory in the church triumphant, so he should want no praise or reverence in the church militant. He was beatified on the 18th of April, 1622, and his office is celebrated in the convents of his order on the 19th of October.

sos de sæculo, et a viis vestris pravis recedentes excepit mox amaritudo et confusio animi pœnitentis, ac velut recentium adhuc vulnerum dolor nimius excruciat perturbat. Securæ manus vestræ distillant myrrhæ amaritudinem in salubrem hanc unctionem; "quia cor contritum et humiliatum Deus non despiciet."—D. Bernard. in Cantica sermo. 10. I say if such a conversion be so pleasing to God, how glorious may we judge this holy Father's penance to be, who from his cradle to his grave, lived innocently and austerely? So that we may justly say of him as the Church of St. John, "Antra deserti teneris sub annis, civium turmas fugiens petisti, ne levi saltem maculare vitam, flamine posses."

BENEDICTUS DEUS.

BEATIFICATIO
B. P.
DE ALCANTARA.

GREGORIUS PAPA XV. AD PERPETUAM REI MEMORIAM.

In Sede Principis Apostolorum, nullis licet nostris suffragantibus meritis, a Domino constituti, piis fidelium votis, quibus virtutum Dominus in servis suis honorificatur, libenter annuimus, eaque favoribus prosequimur opportunis. Cum itaque, instantibus non solum claræ memoriæ Philippo III. et charissimo in Christo filio nostro Philippo IV. Hispaniarum Regibus Catholicis, sed etiam fere omnibus Hispaniæ regnis, venerabiles fratres nostri S. R. E. Cardinales sacris ritibus præpositi, de mandato nostro causam servi Dei, Petri de Alcantara Ord. Minorum, strictioris observantiæ Discalceatorum nuncupatorum, ac Provinciæ S. Josephi ejusdem Ordinis Fundatoris, juxta seriem relationis trium causarum Palatii Apostolici Auditorum ad effectum canonizationis pluries examinaverint, ac multis desuper habitis sessionibus referente dilecto filio nostro Marco Antonio, tituli S. Eusebii Presbytero Cardinale Gonzadino nuncupato, plenissime constare de validitate processuum, ſama sanctitatis, fide, puritate, cæterisque virtutibus non in genere solum, sed etiam in specie, reliquiarum ac sepulchri veneratione, plurimisque tandem miraculis pronunciaverint, censueritque posse Nos quandocumque voluerimus, eumdem Dei servum, juxta Catholicæ Ecclesiæ ritum, Sanctum atque in cælis regnantem declarare omnibusque fidelibus solemni canonizatione proponere venerandum. Prædictus vero Philippus IV. Rex et dilecti filii Minister Generalis, et Fratres Ordinis prædicti Nobis humiliter supplicari fecerunt, ut donec ad canonizationem dicti Petri deveniatur, idem Petrus Beatus nuncupari ac de eo tamquam de Confessore non Pont. Missa, ac officium ut infra celebrari recitari, respective possit, indulgere de benignitate Apostolica dignaremur. Nos supplicationibus hujusmodi inclinati de eorumdem Cardinalium consilio ut idem Dei servus Petrus de Alcantara in posterum Beatus nuncupari, atque de eo tamquam de Confessore non Pontifice die 19, Octob. qua ipsius obitus memoria celebrabitur ubique terrarum ab universa Religione Minorum Observantium utriusque sexus respective Missa celebrari, atque officium recitari possit. In oppido vero de Alcantara nullius diœcesis ubi natus atque in altero de Arenas Abulensis diœcesis, ubi corpus ejusdem requiescere accepimus, omnibus tam regularibus quam secularibus Clericis, sub ritu tamen semiduplici eidem omnino liceat. Ac demum in

Provincia prædicta Sancti Josephi, eujus auctor extitit, ab ipsis dicti Ordinis Discalceatorum fratribus, etiam cum octava veluti de Patrono, officium pariter ac Missa juxta Breviarii, ac Missalis Romani rubricas celebrari possint, Apostolica auctoritate tenore præsentium perpetuo concedimus et indulgemus. Non obstantibus Constitutionibus et ordinationibus Apostolicis, cæterisque contrariis quibuscumque. Volumus autem, ut præsentium transumptis etiam impressis manu alicujus Notarii Publici subscriptis, et sigillo personæ in dignitate Ecclesiastica constitutæ munitis eadem prorsus fides ubique adhibeatur, quæ præsentibus adhiberetur si forent exhibitæ vel ostensæ. Datum Romæ apud S. Petrum sub annulo Piscatoris, die 18 Aprilis, 1622. Pontificatus nostri anno secundo.

Copia veradesumpta ex tomo 3. Bullarii Laertii Cherubini.

FACULTAS SUPERIORIS.

LIBRUM vere pium Meditationum BEATI PETRI DE ALCANTARA, Ordinis Fratr. Min. in linguam Anglicanam a religioso Patre Fr. *Ægidio Willoughby*, ejusdem Ordinis Provinciæ nostræ Angl. filio, fideliter translatum, per omnia concordantem exemplari Latino invenerunt R. R. P. P. Theologi, quibus a nobis commissa fuit ejusdem examinatio, ideoque prælo dignum censuit ad instructionem populi Christiani, qui in tot controversiis fidei, his piis majorum nostrorum exercitiis pene destituitur. Habet insuper adjunctam vitam ipsius BEATI PATRI e variis authoribus a prædicto Patre *Ægidio* collectam, de qua idem sit judicium. Dat. in nostra residentia Londini, 1 Aprilis 1632.

Fr. JOANNES GENINGES,
Minister Provincialis.

APPROBATIO.

MEDITATIONES hæ BEATI PETRI DE ALCANTARA, in linguam Anglicanam a Religioso Patre Fr. *Ægidio Willoughby*, Ordinis Minorum Sti. FRANCISCI translatæ, uti et vita dicti Beati Patris ab eodem auctore ex probatis auctoribus collecta, lucem videre merentur. Actum hac 10 Aprilis 1632.

HENRICUS CALENUS,

St. Theol. Licent. Archipr.

Brux. Librorum Censor.

A

GOLDEN TREATISE

OF

MENTAL PRAYER.

COMPOSED BY THE REVEREND AND HOLY FATHER FR. PETER DE ALCANTARA, OF THE SERAPHICAL ORDER OF ST. FRANCIS.

CHAPTER I.

In this Chapter we will briefly set down the fruit of prayer and meditation, that men considering the benefit of them, may be incited with a prompt and more willing mind to frequent these holy exercises.

It is most certain, that the malice of our own hearts, is the principal cause that hindereth us from attaining to our beatitude and everlasting happiness, because it maketh us slow to godly actions, dull to virtuous exercises, and suggesteth a greater difficulty in them than there is, which if it were not, a man might walk without any molestation in the way of virtue, and at length without labor attain to his desired end. Hence, it is, that the Apostle saith: "*I am delighted with the law of God according to* *the inward man: but I see another law in my members fighting against the law of my mind, and captivating me in the law of sin."*[*]

The efficacy of devotion. This, therefore, is the prime root and cause of all our miseries, against which there is no remedy more convenient and efficacious than devotion, which, according to St. Thomas, is nothing else, but a certain promptitude and facility of the mind to do well. It doth exclude from our mind this tedious difficulty, and maketh us with alacrity apply ourselves to virtuous acts. Therefore, not without cause we may term it spiritual food, recreative and heavenly dew, a pleasant instinct and supernatural affection of the Holy Ghost, which doth so strengthen and transform the hearts of men, that it doth beget in them a new gust and feeling of spiritual things, and on the contrary, a tedious loathing of worldly vanities.

Daily experience manifesteth this particular unto us. For we see the souls of those who arise from profound and devout prayer, to be strengthened with admirable resolutions, adorned with new graces, and replenished with firm purposes of amendment of life, and frequenting pious exercises, they burn with an ardent desire of serving and loving him with their whole heart, whom in their prayer they found the God of all goodness and benignity, desiring

* Rom. vii. 22.

to suffer any grievous and burdensome cross whatsoever it be, yea to shed their blood for his sake. To conclude, prayer is a bath, an open place, a bed of pleasure, wherein the soul recreateth and refresheth herself.

By what means devotion is gotten.

If you ask me what be the chiefest means to attain unto this heroical virtue of devotion, I answer with the same Doctor, that it is gotten by serious meditation, and contemplation of heavenly things. For the ruminating of these in the soul, with a more attentive and profound consideration, doth beget in the will that disposition which we call devotion, which effectually rouseth and pricketh a man forward to every good work. For this cause, the exercise of prayer and meditation was frequent and familiar to men of sanctity, as judging it the easiest means to compass devotion, which, although it be but one only simple virtue, yet it disposeth, and maketh us fit for all others, and as it were with spurs pricketh us forward to the performance of every good work.

I call St. Bonaventure to witness what I say: his words are these.* The inestimable virtue of prayer is able to obtain all good, and remove all hurtful things. If thou wilt patiently endure adversity, be a man of prayer. If thou wilt overcome tribulation and tempta-

* Bonaventure in the Meditation of the life of Christ. cap. 73.

tions, be a man of prayer. If thou wilt trample upon thy perverse inclinations, be a man of prayer. If thou wilt know the deceits of Satan, and avoid them, be a man of prayer. If thou wilt live joyfully in the work of God, and trace the way of labor and affliction, be a man of prayer. If thou wilt exercise thyself in a spiritual course, and not walk according to the desires of the flesh, be a man of prayer. If thou wilt put to flight thy vain and trifling fancies, be a man of prayer. If thou wilt feast thy soul with holy thoughts, good desires, fervor, and devotion, be a man of prayer. If thou wilt establish thy heart with a manly spirit, and constant purpose in the service of God, be a man of prayer. To conclude, if thou wilt root out vice, and be endued with virtues, be a man of prayer. In it is received the unction of the Holy Ghost, which teacheth all things. Also, if thou wilt climb up to the top of contemplation, and enjoy the sweet embracings of thy beloved spouse, be a man of prayer. For by the exercise of prayer, we come to that contemplation and taste of heavenly things. Thou seest of what great power and virtue prayer is. For the confirmation of all which, omitting the testimony of holy Scriptures, let this be an evident proof unto thee, that by daily experience, we hear and see illiterate and simple persons, to have attained the aforesaid, and greater things by the virtue of prayer. Thus St. Bonaventure.

I beseech you, can there be found a richer treasure, or a more fertile field desired? Hear another Doctor no less for religion and sanctity, who upon the same matter saith: by prayer the soul is cleansed from sin, replenished with charity, confirmed in faith, strengthened, and refreshed in spirit. Prayer establisheth the inward man, pacifieth the heart, knoweth the truth, conquereth temptations, expelleth sorrow, reneweth the senses, stirreth up languishing virtue, putteth to flight tepidity, and scoureth the rust of vices. In prayer, the quick sparkles of celestial desires are incessantly sent forth, from the burning coals of divine love. The privileges of prayer are rare, the prerogatives admirable. Prayer unlocketh the gates of heaven, manifesteth divine secrets, and always findeth free access to the ears of God. I will add no more, for those things which have already been said, abundantly express the fruits of this holy exercise.

CHAPTER II.

OF THE MATTER OF PRAYER.

HAVING taken notice of the utility of prayer and meditation, we will now declare the matter about which meditation is to be conversant; for seeing it is ordained to this end, that the soul of him that meditateth, may be excited to the fear and love of God, and the keeping of his commandments; the matter of meditation ought to be such, as doth next dispose to this end, and scope. And, although every creature, and the whole Scripture itself be able to minister this matter unto us, yet speaking generally, the mysteries of our holy faith, contained in the *Creed*, are most efficacious and profitable to attain unto this end. For these on the one side, contain Almighty God's benefits, the latter judgment, the pains of hell, and the glory of paradise; all which, like sharp pricks, do spur us on to the love and fear of God. On the other side, they comprehend the life and passion of our Lord and Saviour, which is the spring and fountain of all our good. These two things contained in the Apostolical *Creed*, for the most part yield matter of meditation; and, therefore, I think, prayer and meditation ought chiefly to be conversant about them, although every one in particular may have certain points, which may more specially inflame and excite the soul to the love and fear of God.

Being, therefore, persuaded with this reason, that I might the better conduct young beginners, and untrained soldiers into this way of mental prayer, and that I might give unto them altogether prepared, and (as it were to little children) foreshowed matter of meditation; I have selected two kinds of meditations, almost taken out of the mysteries of our faith; the one serving for the morning, the other for the evening; that as the body is commonly fed with two meals, so the soul may be strengthened and nourished with two spiritual refections, by the meditation and consideration of heavenly things. Some of these are of the passion and resurrection of our Lord Jesus Christ, others of the mysteries of our faith, as I said before. But those who cannot have the opportunity, to meditate twice-a-day, after this manner, they may use them, to wit, they may take to their consideration the seven former meditations in the one week, and the latter in another week; or they may chiefly insist upon those of the life and passion of our Saviour; although the other be not to be neglected, especially in the beginning of a soul's conversion, to whom they are proper, when the fear of God, contrition and horror of sin, is chiefly to be regarded and sought after.

HERE FOLLOW THE SEVEN FORMER MEDITATIONS.

A MEDITATION FOR MONDAY.

THIS day thou shalt call to memory thy sins, and shalt exercise thyself in the knowledge of thyself, that on the one side thou mayest truly ponder the greatness of thy offences, and on the other side, thou mayest look into thy baseness, and thy own nothing, and acknowledge that all the good which thou hast, is from God. This consideration will get thee submission of mind, and true humility, the mother of all virtues.

First, therefore, weigh with thyself, the multitude of the sins of thy former life, and namely, those sins which thou hast committed, when as yet thou wert not illuminated with the divine splendor to know Almighty God rightly. These if thou dost examine with exquisite diligence, thou wilt find to be so many in number, that they will exceed the hairs of thy head; for in this time thou leadest the life of a heathen, ignorant of the divine power, and as it were without any knowledge of his sacred Deity.

Then consider how thou hast behaved thyself about the ten commandments, and the seven deadly sins, and thou wilt find, that there is no precept of Almighty God, which thou hast not violated, nor any mortal sin, into which thou hast not fallen, either in thought, word, or deed. After that, call to mind Almighty God's benefits, which he hath bestowed upon thee in the whole course of thy former life, and see whether thou canst give a good account of them or no.

Tell me, I pray thee, how thou hast consumed the days of thy infancy, thy youth, and the flower of thy manly age? how hast thou employed thy five exterior senses, and inward faculties of thy soul, given unto thee by God, only to be busied about his holy service, and the contemplation of heavenly things; what hast thou turned thine eyes unto, but to behold vanities? what have thine ears listened after, but lies and tales? what hath thy tongue uttered, but murmurings and blasphemous speeches? what hath thy taste and feeling been delighted in, but wanton pleasures? how hast thou used the remedy of the holy Sacraments, given unto thee as a singular gift? what thanksgiving hast thou restored for so many benefits which he hath heaped upon thee? what alacrity hast thou used to satisfy his holy inspirations? how hast thou spent thy health of body and natural forces? how hast thou dispensed thy goods of fortune? what good use hast thou made of the commodity, and proffered occasions to live well? what care hast thou had of thy neighbor's welfare?

what works of mercy, or of bounty, hast thou done unto them? what wilt thou answer in that terrible day of judgment, when thou must render a severe account of all these things! O withered tree, destinated to eternal flames, except thou dost penance! what excuse wilt thou then frame, when thou must give an account of every year, of every month, of every week, of every day, of every moment!

Thirdly, consider, those sins, which thou hast every day committed, after Almighty God hath illuminated and opened the eyes of thy soul to meditate upon heavenly things; and thou shalt find that the old *Adam* hath yet borne a great sway in thy actions, and that sinful root to have procreated in thee, many and perverse habits.

Diligently ponder, how ungrateful thou hast been to Almighty God, how unmindful of his benefits, how contrary thou hast behaved thyself against his holy inspirations, how slothful and remiss in his divine service; in which thou scarce hast ever used due alacrity and diligence, or such purity of intention as is requisite, nay, hast thou not served God for worldly respects and commodity?

Enter into consideration how rigid thou art to thy neighbor, and how indulgent to thyself? how thou lovest thy own will, how thou adherest to thy sensuality, how chary of thy honor, and of every thing that belongeth unto thee. Weigh well with thyself, how every day thou growest more arrogant, more ambitious, more vain, more prone to anger, more desperately bent to malice, more prone to delights and pleasures, more mutable, more unconstant, more propense to carnal sins and a greater lover of earthly vanities. Consider thy inconstancy in good, thy indiscretion in words, imprudence in deeds, in high and difficult matters pusillanimity sometimes, and often audacious temerity.

In the fourth place, after thou hast taken notice of the number and order of thy sins, pause upon them a while in thy mind, and weigh every one in the balance of due consideration, that thou mayest perceive with what misery thou art on every side environed. Which, that thou mayest the better do; consider these three circumstances in the sins of thy former life. First, against whom thou hast sinned. Second, why thou hast sinned. Third, how thou hast sinned. Which, if thou dost diligently penetrate, thou wilt find that thou hast offended God, whose majesty and goodness is immense, who hath obliged man unto him with so many benefits, as there are sands in the sea, or drops of water in the ocean.

Why hast thou sinned, or what violent occasion hath enforced thee to any crime? a little momentary pride; a foul representation of pleasure; some small commodity placed in thy sight, and oftentimes no occasion at all, but evil custom, and mere contempt of God.

But alas, how hast thou sinned? with such facility, with such notable audacity, with so little fear and conscience, yea with such serenity and pleasure, as though thou hadst to do with no other than a wooden God, who regardeth not these sublunary things, neither understandeth nor seeth any thing what is done on the face of earth. Is this the honor due unto his supreme majesty? is this a renumeration of his benefits? dost thou with such services requite his whippings, his buffetings, and precious blood shed upon the cross for thy sake? O wicked wretch, that hast offended so great a majesty, more miserable, that for so slight a cause, and most deplorable, that thou art not sensible of thy utter ruin: that after sin thou fearest not damnation, and so neglectest to do penance.

Moreover, it is very profitable, to insist a while upon this consideration, and that thou esteem thyself nothing, and certainly persuade thyself that thou hast nothing of thyself but sin; all other things to be the gifts of Almighty God's bounty. For it is most evident, that all our good, both of grace and nature doth flow from him; for he is the author of the grace of predestination (which is the fountain and original of all others) of the grace of our vocation, of concomitant and preserving grace, and of the grace of everlasting life. What hast thou then, that thou canst boast of, but sin? only this, nothing thou canst attribute to thyself, all other things belong to God: whence thou mayest clearly and manifestly perceive what he is, and what thou art, and hence conjecture, what diffidence thou oughtest to have in thyself, and what confidence in God, to love him, and to glorify thyself in him, and not in thyself, but so far as his grace doth freely operate in thee.

These things being digested with attentive meditation, as much as thou canst, urge thyself to a contempt of thyself: imagine that thou art like an empty reed, shaken with every blast of wind, without gravity, without virtue, without constancy, without stability, and, finally, without any thing. Think thyself to be a *Lazarus*, four days dead, a stinking and abominable carcass, swarming with vermin, so filthy that passers by, are forced to stop their nostrils, lest they smell such a nasty savour. Believe me, thou art more abominable before God and his holy saints. Think thyself unworthy to lift up thine eyes to heaven; to tread upon the earth, or that the creatures should serve thee; yea, not worthy to eat bread or breathe in the air. Cast thyself, with the sinful women in the gospel, at our Blessed Saviour's feet; presenting thyself unto him with a confused and blushing countenance, no otherwise than the woman taken in adultery before her husband, and with inward sorrow and true compunction, beg pardon for thy sins; that, for his infinite mercy and goodness, he would vouchsafe to receive thee again into his favor, and that thou mayest dwell in his house for ever.

A MEDITATION FOR TUESDAY.

This day thou shalt meditate upon the miseries of the life of man, out of which consideration, thou wilt take notice of worldly vanities, and learn how much glory of them ought to be despised, seeing they are built upon so weak a foundation as our fading life, whose miseries, because they be innumerable, thou shalt take but seven of the principal for thy meditation.

First, therefore, consider the shortness of the life of man, being restrained within the limits of threescore and ten, or fourscore years, whatsoever the overplus be, it is but labor and sorrow, as the Prophet speaketh: Out of this time, if thou dost subtract thy infancy, which time thou didst live rather the life of a beast than a man; the time thou spendest in sleep, for then thou art deprived of the use of reason, which only distinguisheth man from other creatures, and thou wilt find thy life to be far shorter than ever thou didst imagine. This time if thou dost compare with the eternity of the world to come, thou wilt find it to be less than a moment. Conjecture, then, the foolish madness of the lovers of this world, who, that they might enjoy one only momentary pleasure of this transitory life, do not fear to expose themselves to the loss of eternity.

Then take to thy consideration the uncertainty of this life, (which is a second misery) for not only it is most short, but the brevity itself is most uncertain and doubtful. For who is there, that attaineth to the age of three, or four score? how many are extinguished at their very entrance into the world? how many perish in the flower of their youth? You know it not, saith Christ, when your Lord is to come; whether in the first watch, or second, or third, or in the cock-crowing. Which, that thou mayest the better understand, call to mind especially thy domestic friends, and other men placed in dignity and authority, whom inexorable death have, at divers ages, (some younger, some older) suddenly taken out of this world, dissipating their vain and long-life promising hopes.

Ponder, fourthly, the inconstancy and mutability of this present life, never continuing in one state. The disposition of the body often changeth, not always enjoying health, but subject to frequent diseases; but if thou reflect upon the mind, thou shalt see, that, like the troubled ocean, it is tossed up and down with the boisterous winds of her untamed passions, inordinate appetites, fluctuating cogitations, which upon every occasion do disturb her quiet. Consider, lastly, the instability of the goods of fortune, as they term them, to how many chances they are obnoxious, never suffering the temporal substance to stand still in one stay, thereby to make men happy and prosperous; but, like a wheel, is turned upside down, without any intermission. Consider, also, the continual motion of our life, never resting night nor day, but goeth forward without ceasing, and every day more and more wasteth itself; so that it may not unfitly be compared to a candle, which, by little and little, consumeth itself, and when it giveth the clearest light, the sooner it approacheth unto its end; also to a flower, which springeth up in the morning, at noon fadeth, and at night wholly withereth away. Which Almighty God, speaking by the Prophet Isaiah of this mutation, excellently shadoweth in these words: "*Omnis caro fœnum, et omnis gloria ejus quasi flos agri:*" "All flesh is hay, and all the glory of it is like the flower of the field."

Which words, St. Jerome expounding, saith:* If one doth rightly consider the frailty of the flesh, and that we grow and decrease according to the moments of hours; never remaining in one state, and that the very thing we now speak, do, or write, passeth away as part of our life, he will not doubt to confess that all flesh is hay, and the glory thereof as a flower, or the green meadows. He that is now an infant will, by and by, be a little child, then presently a young man, growing towards his decrepid age, through uncertain seasons, and before he hath contented himself in youth, feeleth old age to come upon him. The beau-

* Hieron. l. ii. Com. in Isa. cap. 40.

tiful woman which did draw after her whole troops of gallants in her youth, her face is now furrowed with deformed wrinkles, and she that before was a pleasure, is now ugly to behold.

Consider fifthly, how deceitful this life is, (which is the worst condition of all, deluding the lovers of this world with a miserable blindness,) for we think it amiable, when in itself it is ugly: we think it sweet, when it is full of gall and bitterness: when it is circumscribed within the shortest limits, we think it long. When it is full of misery, we think it so happy, that there is no danger, no hazard, that men will not expose themselves unto, for the conservation of it: yea, with the loss of eternal glory, when they do not fear to commit those sins which make them unworthy of so great felicity.

Consider sixthly, that besides the brevity, and other fore-mentioned conditions, that small time wherein we live, is subject to innumerable miseries, both spiritual and corporal: that it may well be called a torrent of tears, and ocean of infinite molestations. St. Jerome reporteth how Xerxes, that potent king, who overturned mountains, and made bridges over the seas, when, from a high place, he beheld that infinite multitude of men, and his innumerable army, he wept, to think that not one of those men there present, should be alive after a hundred years. And presently adding, O that we could but ascend into such a turret, to behold the whole earth under our feet, then would I manifest unto thee, the ruins of the world; nation rising against nation, and kingdom against kingdom; some tormented, others slain, some drowned, others led into captivity. Here marrying, here mourning, some born, others dying, some abounding in wealth, others begging. And not only the mighty army of Xerxes, but all the men of the world, in a short space, to be turned to dust and ashes.

Take notice, a little of the labors and infirmities of the body, the cogitations and passions of the mind; the diverse dangers in every state, and all seasons threatening the ruin of man; and thou wilt every day, more clearly understand the miseries of this life, that when thou seest what is to be hoped for in this world, thou mayest with a noble courage contemn it.

The last of all these miseries, is death, both in respect of soul or body, a thing most terrible, for in this moment the body is disrobed of all things in this world. And the soul in this point receiveth the joyful or fearful sentence of eternity.

These things well considered, thou wilt be instructed how short and miserable the glory of this world is, and how it ought to be hated and despised of thee.

A MEDITATION FOR WEDNESDAY.

This day thou shalt meditate on death: the consideration of which, is very profitable to attain unto true wisdom, to beat down sin, and to excite men timely to cast up their accounts, which they are to make in the latter day.

Consider, first, the uncertainty of that hour, wherein death is to seize upon thee, thou knowest not the day, nor the place, nor the state wherein it shall find thee; only thou believest that thou must die, for other things thou art wholly ignorant of, except that it sometimes setteth upon a man when he little dreameth of it, and thinketh it to be furthest of.

Consider, secondly, that grievous separation, which shall be at the point of death, not only from every thing of this present life, wherein thou lookest content, but also betwixt the soul and body, whose society was most ancient, most loving and dear. If a man taketh it grievously to be banished, to be thrust out of his native soil, and to be deprived of that air wherein he first breathed, although he should carry all others, his dearest things with him, how far more bitterly would he take that general exile, wherein he most weaned from all worldly things, his house, his means, his father, his mother, his children, his friends, uncertain whither he himself must go. Then, shall he be deprived of the light and the commerce of all human creatures?

If the ox when he is disjoined from his fellow, with whom he was wont in the same yoke to be coupled, with bellowing doth express his sorrow, what sobs, what sighs wilt thou fetch, when thou shalt perceive thyself to be violently pulled from these thy confederates.

Consider, also, that anxiety wherewith the mind of the dying is tormented, when abstracted from all corporal business, he only thinketh what shall become of his body, and what shall betide his soul, how his body must be cast seven foot into the earth, to be eaten of worms; and what will become of his soul, where it is to remain, he is altogether uncertain; which cogitation doth surely much trouble the mind of him that dieth, when he certainly knoweth there is heaven or hell to be expected, and he, at equal distance, from them both, neither can he tell which of these two contraries will fall to his share.

Another no less affliction followeth, that presently he must give a strict account of all his forepassed life, to the eternal judge, which men of great sanctity were wont to fear, when Arsenius in the last point of life, was seen of his disciples to weep and tremble, they asked him why he feared death, he answered: **Revera filioli, metus hic quo me videtis affici nunquam omnino a me recessit ex quo factus sum Monachus.* Indeed, my children, the fear where-

* Simon Metaph, in vita ejus tome 4, apud Sarium.

with ye see me now afflicted, hath quite left me from the time I was first made a monk.

Then all the sins of a man's former life come rushing into his memory, representing themselves unto him, as it were in battle array, to destroy him, but especially, his grievous sins wherein he took greatest delight, are continually present to his fancy, which do so torment him that they drive him into a dangerous despair of his salvation, and the remembrance of those pleasures, which before were grateful, are now most bitter unto him. That the wise man saith true:* "*Ne intuaris vinum quando flavescit cum splenduerit in vitro color ejus ingreditur blande, et in novissimo mordebit ut coluber, et sicut regulus venema diffundet.*" "Behold not wine when it waxeth yellow, when the color thereof shall shine in the glass; it goeth in pleasantly, but in the end it will bite like a snake, and as a basilisk it spreads abroad his passions."

Such a poisoned cup the enemy of mankind presenteth to the lovers of the world to drink. Such is the liquor of the outward gilded cup of *Babylon*.

Wicked man seeing himself environed with so many accusers, beginneth then to fear the success of his latter judgment, and to bewail himself with bitter outcries, O miserable and unhappy man that have lived thus long in

* Proverbs, xxiii.

darkness, and walked in the footsteps of iniquity, what shall now become of me? if St. Paul saith* such as a man soweth, such he shall reap. I that have sowed nothing else but the works of the flesh, what should I expect but corruption?

If St. John saith, that no unclean thing shall enter into that heavenly city, which is paved with burnished gold, what part shall I have therein, that am defiled with all kind of luxury.

Then follow the sacraments of the church: confession, communion, extreme unction, which are the last helps of our holy mother the Catholic Church, to succor his dying soul.

From all these aforesaid circumstances, thou mayest gather with what anxiety a wicked man is oppressed at the hour of his departure. Then he will wish that he had led a better life, and what great austerity he would use if longer time might be permitted to him. Then would he vehemently implore the divine assistance, but the greatness of his infirmity, and the pangs of death approaching, will not suffer him, which will be so great that he shall scarce be able to turn his thoughts upon God.

Behold, after these, the symptoms of this last infirmity, forerunners of death, and harbingers of thy last end, which certainly in themselves are horrible, and to the beholders terrible. The stomach swelleth, the speech faileth, the

* Galatians, vi.

feet begin to die, the knees wax cold, the nostrils fall, the eyes sink, the face waxeth pale, the tongue can no longer perform its office; finally, the striving of the soul going out of the body, disturbeth all the senses, and leaveth them wholly without vigor.

But who is able to express the anguish of the soul, which is far greater? for then it is in a mighty agony, both in regard of the doubtful event of her salvation, and of the strict account she is presently to make of the deeds of her whole life; as also, because she naturally loveth the body; she cannot be separated from it but with great affliction, especially, knowing not what shall become of her.

Having well contemplated the soul departing the body, thou must yet make two journies more: one in accompanying the body to the grave, the other in following the soul to the deciding of her cause. And thou shalt see the event of both. Mark, therefore, the dead carcass how they prepare a winding sheet for it. What expedition they use to carry it out of the house. Consider the solemnity and rites wherewith it is carried to the grave. How the bells ring, and every one inquire of the dead. The office of the church also, the prayers of the standers by, the doleful tune of the church, while the body is carried to the grave and buried. The tears of friends and kindred, and all those ceremonies which are wont to be performed about the dead.

Leaving the body under the earth, accompany the soul passing to a new and unknown region, where she expecteth the sentence of the eternal judge. Imagine with thyself that thou art present at this tribunal, and the whole court of heaven, waiting with deep silence, and great attention, the event and sentence of this judgment, here must be given a strict account of all receivings and disbursements. I say account, of thy life, of thy goods, of thy family, of the divine inspirations, of the means and occasions to live well, and finally, of the blood of Jesus Christ, and the use of his sacraments, and according as his account is, so the sentence shall be pronounced.

A MEDITATION FOR THURSDAY.

This day thou shalt meditate upon the latter judgment, to the end, that thou mayest stir up in thy soul two principal effects, which every Christian soul ought to have, to wit, the fear of God and hatred of sin.

Place, therefore, first before thine eyes, how terrible that day will be, wherein all the litigious causes of the sons of *Adam* shall be decided, and a final end put to the processes of our whole life, and what shall be ordained of those for all eternity, shall be publicly pronounced to the view of the whole world.

This day comprehendeth in it, all the days of all ages, past, present, and to come; and exacteth a severe account of all the actions of all men, pouring out all the fury upon men, heaped up together from forepassed ages; because then the torrent of Almighty God's vengeance shall overflow beyond its limits, rushing with a greater violence, by how much more it was the longer detained, and at once shall overwhelm all iniquity from the creation of the world.

Consider, secondly, the dreadful signs which shall go before this day. For our Saviour saith: *Erunt signa in sole, et luna, et stellis.** And all creatures of heaven and earth shall tremble, understanding their ruin to be at hand. Men also, as our Saviour saith, worn and withered away, perceiving the horrible raging of the sea; and they, themselves, scarce a hair's breadth distant from death. Seeing also, the mighty risings and inundations of the water; and by these conjecturing the calamities and misery these prodigious signs threaten to the world, will be amazed with such a horror, that they will be without life, without voice, without color, or human shape; they will be dead before they die, dreading their damnation before the sentence be pronounced, imagining the future pain, by their present distemper. Then every one out of exceeding fear, will be so solicitous of himself, that he will nothing regard others whosoever they be,

* Luc. c. xxi. v. 25.

parents, or husbands, or wives, or friends, or companions.

Imagine, thirdly, the universal deluge of fire, which shall go before this judgment; that dreadful noise of the trumpet, which one of the archangels shall blow, wherewith all the people of the whole world shall be summoned together, in one place, making their appearance before the judgment seat; and last of all, that dreadful majesty, the supreme judge of the quick and dead, shall assume to himself upon this tribunal.

Fourthly, consider, what exact account shall be required of every one. Holy Job saith: "*Vere scio quod ita sit: et quod non justificetur homo compositus Deo. Si voluerit contendere cum eo, non poterit ei respondere unum pro mille.*"* "Indeed, I know it is so, and that man cannot be justified, compared with God. If he will contend with him, he cannot answer him one for a thousand." What then shall become of man, when God shall begin to handle him according to the rigor of his justice, when he shall speak to his conscience inwardly?

O wicked and perverse man, what hast thou seen in me, that out of the height of impiety, despising me, thou shouldst join with my enemies? I have created thee according to mine own image and likeness: I have illuminated thee with the light of faith: I have seasoned

* Job, c. ix. v. 23.

thee in the Christian faith from thy infancy: I have redeemed thee with my own blood: for thy sake I have fasted, watched, prayed, undergone tedious journies, sweat blood, and endured many more miseries in the course of my life: for the love of thee, I have suffered persecutions, injuries, blasphemies, and the very cross itself. This cross is my witness, these nails my witnesses, which thou seest imprinted in my hands and feet: to conclude, heaven and earth that did behold my passion are my witnesses. How I have drawn thy soul. How I have redeemed thee with the ransom of my precious blood.

How hast thou esteemed this precious pearl? bought by me with an inestimable price. O generation of vipers, why hast thou chosen to serve my enemy with a great deal of pain, and neglected thy duty towards me, thy Creator, and Redeemer, which thou mightest have performed with a great deal of pleasure. I have called thee, and thou wouldst not answer to my vocation. I have knocked at the door of thy heart, and thou hast refused me entrance. I have stretched my arms upon the cross, and thou hast not regarded me, thou despiseth my counsels, promises, and threatenings. Pronounce, therefore, O ye angels, the sentence, and be judges betwixt me and my vineyard. "*Quid est quod debui uttra facere vineæ meæ ut non feci ei?*" "What is there that I ought to do more to my vineyard, that I have not done to it."*

What will the reprobate and scoffers at divine mysteries answer? they that have hissed at virtue, derided simplicity, and observed better the laws of the world than of God; they that have stopped their ears at the voice of God; they who have contemned his divine inspirations; they who have been rebellious against his commandments, and ungrateful for his benefits. What will those libertines say, who letting themselves loose to all vices, have lived as if there were no God at all, or that he did not regard the things that are done below. What will those say, who have followed their commodities, gust, and pleasure for a law. "*Quid facietis in die visitationis et calamitatis de longe venientis, ad cujus confuegietis auxilium? et ubi derelinquetis gloriam vestram ut non incurvimini sub vinculo et cum interfectis cadatis?*" "What will ye do in the day of visitation and of calamity coming from afar? To whose help will ye flee, and where will ye leave your glory, that ye be not bowed under the bond, and fall with the slain?"

Fifthly, consider, that terrible sentence, which, after judgment, the supreme Judge pronounceth against the wicked; which he will thunder out with such a dreadful noise, that at the sound thereof, the ears of the standers by

* Isaias, c. v. v. 3, 4.

will ring, as the prophet Isaias saith :* "*Labia ejus repleta sunt indignatione, et lingua ejus quasi ignis devorans.*" "His lips are filled with indignation, and his tongue as a devouring fire." For what flames can be so ardent as those words: "*Discedite a me maledicti in ignum æternum, qui paratus est Diabolo et angelis ejus.*" "Go from me, O ye cursed into everlasting fire, prepared for the Devil and his angels." Every word of which sentence, is full of bitter torment. For who is able to comprehend what this separation is, what curse, what fire, what society, and, finally, what eternity, to which the wicked are adjudged by force of this sentence?

A MEDITATION FOR FRIDAY.

This day thou shalt meditate upon the torments of hell, that duly pondering them, thou mayest have more awe of Almighty God, and a greater hatred of sin. St. Bonaventure† teacheth, that these torments are to be considered according to certain similitudes set down by holy men, concerning this matter. Wherefore, it will not be beside our purpose (as the same Doctor, in the same place saith,) to imagine hell a horrible confused chaos, a lake under the earth, a deep fiery dungeon; or as a spacious city, dark and terrible, burning with

* Isaias, c. xxx. v. 27.
† D. Bonaven. in Fas. cap. 3.

obscure and fearful fire, filled with wailings, howlings, weeping, for the inexplicable pains.

In this miserable and unhappy place, are two kinds of torments, *pœna sensus, et pœna damni,* the punishment of sense, and the punishment of loss of Almighty God.

Consider that there is no outward or inward sense of the damned, which is not afflicted with a proper torment; for as the damned, in all their members and senses, have offended God, using them as instruments and weapons whereby, neglecting the society and law of God, they served sin, so the divine justice hath ordained that every sense, according to their desert, should be tormented with a proper punishment; the wanton and lascivious eyes, shall be tortured with the hideous aspect of devils. The ears which were open to lies, detractions, and other impurities, shall ring with unwonted clamors, outcries, and blasphemies. The noses which were delighted with sweet odors shall be poisoned with an intolerable stink. The taste which was glutted with dainty fare, shall be tormented with intolerable hunger and thirst. The tongue which uttered detractions and murmurings, shall drink the gall of dragons. The wanton, which gave consent to their brutish desires, shall be frozen with extreme cold, and as holy Job saith:* "*Ad nimium calorem transeat ab aquis nivium:*"

* Job, c. v. v. 24.

"Let him pass from the snow waters to excessive heat."

The interior senses also shall not want their torments, the imagination shall not be tormented with the apprehension of present pains, the memory with the calling to mind of forepast pleasures, the understanding with the fear of future griefs, the will with an incredible hatred and raging towards God.

There, as St. Gregory saith, shall be intolerable cold, unquenchable fire, a never dying worm, a stench which none is able to endure, horrid darkness, grievous whippings, visages of devils, confusion of sinners, and desperation of all good.

Tell me, I pray thee, couldst thou endure one little moment the least part of these torments? surely it would be very grievous, if not intolerable for thee. What then will it be to suffer this whole inundation of evils, at one time in all thy members and senses, external and internal, not one or a thousand nights, but for all eternity? What sense, what tongue, what mind of man is able to conceive or express these things?

Neither are these the greatest torments the damned suffer. There remaineth yet a more grievous, which the divines do call the punishment of loss, which consisteth in the perpetual privation of the beatifical vision of God and his saints, and of all that glorious and blessed society. For that is the greatest torment that depriveth man of the most excellent good. Seeing, therefore, that God is that effectual and chief good of all goods, to be deprived of him must needs be the greatest of all evils.

These are the general torments of the damned; besides these, there are other particular torments, wherewith every one according to their sins are afflicted. The proud, the envious, the covetous, the luxurious, and other vicious have their peculiar torments; the measure of pain there, shall be proportionable to their glory and pleasure here; poverty and want to plenty, hunger and thirst to gluttony and to former delights.

To all these aforesaid torments, eternity is yet to be added, which is, as it were, the seal and key of all the rest; for if at length they should have an end, they were some way tolerable. That which is restrained to a certain time cannot be so insufferable; but this punishment is everlasting, without solace, without relaxation, without diminution, where remaineth no hope of an end of their torments, or tormentors, or themselves that suffer them, but is, as it were, a perpetual and irrevocable banishment, never to be recalled, which is a thing of importance to be noted, that the mind may be stirred up thereby, to that saving fear and love of God.

From the eternity of torments proceedeth that great hatred wherewith they are incensed against God. Hence proceed these horrible blasphemies and curses, which with their impure mouths they rail at God, saying, cursed be God who hath created us, and hath condemned us to an everlasting death, which doth so oppress and torment us, that notwithstanding never killeth. Cursed be his power, which doth so grievously afflict us. Cursed be his wisdom, that hath laid open all our wickedness. Cursed be his justice, that hath exacted eternal punishment for temporal sins. Cursed be his cross, which hath not benefitted us. Cursed be his blood, that was shed, seeing it requireth revenge against us. Cursed be the Mother of God, who although she be pious and propitious to all, yet notwithstanding hath showed herself to us cruel and unmerciful. Cursed be all the saints of God reigning with Christ, and rejoicing at our miseries.

These are the hymns, this is that harsh melody, which the damned do continually jar, railing at the Almighty God with detested blasphemies for all eternity.

A MEDITATION FOR SATURDAY.

This day thou shalt meditate upon the glory of the saints of God, which may more eagerly inflame thy soul, to contemn the vanities of this world, and aspire to that eternal felicity.

To the end thou mayest get a better knowledge and gust of this inestimable glory, consider these five things. First, the excellency of the place. Secondly, the joy of that society. Thirdly, the vision of God. Fourthly, the glory of their bodies. Fifthly, the complete perfection of all abundant good.

In the excellency of the place, take notice of the admirable and wonderful spaciousness of it; in approved authors thou readest, that the least of the fixed stars of heaven, is bigger than the whole earth, and some of them do exceed the earth two or three hundred times in bigness. Then cast up thine eyes to heaven, and consider the innumerable multitude of them in the firmament, and thou shalt see a great deal of void space, where many more may be placed, how canst thou then but be astonished at the greatness of so rare a fabric.

Then consider the beauty of that place, which no tongue is able to express, for if Almighty God, in this place of banishment and vale of misery, hath made many things of admirable and comely hue; of what great beauty, and how much adorned dost thou think that place to be, which God would have to be the ordinary seat of his glory, the palace of his majesty, the mansion of the elect, and the paradise of all pleasure?

After the beauty of the place, consider the nobility of the inhabitants, whose number, sanctity, riches, and glory, are far beyond our imagination. St. John saith, the multitude are so great that they are innumerable. St. Dionysius affirmeth, that the multitude of angels do far exceed the number of sublunary creatures. Whom St. Thomas following, thinketh, that as the heavens by many degrees exceed the bigness of the earth, being but, as it were, a point of them; so proportionably the glorious spirits therein contained, do surpass all earthly things. What can be thought more admirable? assuredly this well pondered would make a man lose himself in the abyss of Almighty God's goodness.

Yea, without comparison every one of these blessed spirits is far more beautiful to the eye than all this visible world. Oh, what would it be to contemplate the incomprehensible number of so rare and glorious spirits, and to understand their several offices and perfections?—How the angels bring messages; how the archangels minister; how the principalities triumph; how the powers rejoice; how the dominations bear sway; how the virtues shine; how the thrones do glitter; how the cherubim do illuminate; how the seraphim do burn with love; and finally, how all with one unanimous consent, do praise Almighty God.

If the conversation and fellowship of good men be so delightful, what pleasure will it be, to be associated with so great a multitude of saints?—to be conversant with the Apostles, to talk with the prophets, to discourse with martyrs, and to enjoy the blessed familiarity of all the elect? Oh, but what will it be to enjoy his presence whom the morning stars do magnify?—whose beauty the sun and moon admire; before whom the holy angels and all the celestial spirits do prostrate themselves. That *summum bonum*, that infinite good, which in itself comprehendeth all good whatsoever; oh, what content will the heart of man feel, to behold him, who is one and all: who although he be most simple without composition, yet containeth in himself the perfections of all things created. What can the heart of man desire greater?

If it were so much to see and hear king Solomon, that the queen of Saba coming from far remote parts, moved with his great wisdom, should say, "*Beati viri tui, et beati servi tui, qui stant coram te semper et audiunt sapientiam tuam:*"* "Blessed are thy men, and blessed are thy servants, who stand before thee always and hear thy wisdom." What would it be to behold that true Solomon, that eternal wisdom, that immense majesty, that inestimable beauty, that infinite goodness? and, which is more, to enjoy him for all eternity.

This is the essential and truest glory of the saints; this is the last end and centre of all our wishes. Consider, moreover, the glory of their bodies, which shall be beautified with these four gifts: subtility, agility, impassibility, and clarity; which will be so great, that every one of the elect, as our blessed Saviour saith, shall glitter like the sun in the kingdom of his father.

If one only sun doth so rejoice and illuminate this universe, what dost thou think so many brighter suns will do, which shall there shine?

* 3 Reg. c. x. v. 8.

What should I speak of other joys which there shall be? health without infirmity, liberty without violence, beauty without deformity, immortality without corruption, abundance without want, rest without trouble, security without fear, riches without poverty, joy without sorrow, honor without contradiction. There, as St. Augustine saith,* shall be true glory, when every one shall be commended without error or flattery. True honor shall be denied to none that is worthy of it, and it shall be given to none unworthy, neither shall any unworthy attempt it there, where none shall be permitted but the worthy. There shall be true peace, where they shall suffer no contradiction from themselves or others; the reward of virtue shall be he which gave virtue. And he hath promised to give himself, than which nothing can be better, or greater. For what other thing is it, that he spake by the prophet: "*Ero illorum Deus, et ipsi erunt mihi plebs*:" "I will be their God, and they shall be my people." If I do not, who is it that can satiate their souls? I will be that good which can possibly be desired of man, their life, their peace, their honor. For so is that understood which the Apostle speaketh: "*Ut sit Deus in omnibus*:" "that God be in all." He shall be the end of all our desires, which shall be contemplated without end, shall be loved without tediousness, shall be praised without ceasing.

* D. August. l. 22. de Civit. Dei. cap. 30.

The place of the saints, if thou dost behold the spaciousness of it, it shall be most ample, if the beauty, most delicious; if the splendor, most exceedingly bright. There shall be admirable delightful society, no vicissitude of times, the day shall not succeed the night, nor the night the day, but all time shall be there alike. There shall be one perpetual spring, which the Holy Ghost, with a wonderful temper, shall always make green and flourishing; there shall all celebrate everlasting holidays, rejoicing with unspeakable gladness; there shall all sound their instruments of music and sing praises to him, by whose power they live and reign for all eternity.

O celestial city, secure habitation, palace flowing with all delights, people without murmuring, quiet citizens, men without poverty. Oh, that I may at length enjoy thee. Oh, that the days of my banishment were ended. When will that joyful day come? When shall I go out of this mortality? When shall I come and appear before thy face, O God.

A MEDITATION FOR SUNDAY.

This day thou shalt spend in recogitating Almighty God's benefits, that thou mayest be grateful to him for the same, and thy heart inflamed with the love of him, that hath heaped so many favors upon thee; which seeing they be innumerable, thou shalt take four of the chief to thy consideration, which are, the benefits of thy creation, preservation, redemption, and vocation, besides particular benefits specially bestowed upon thee.

Touching the benefit of thy creation, examine diligently what thou wert before, what God hath given thee when thou hadst no precedent merits. Behold thy comely body well composed of its members and senses; look upon thy noble soul, beautified with these excellent faculties, the understanding, will, and memory.

Remember, that when he gave thee thy soul, he gave thee all things, seeing there is no perfection in any creature, which is not found more excellent in the soul of man. Hence it manifestly followeth, that when God bestowed this great benefit upon thee, he with it bestowed what else soever thou hast.

Concerning the benefit of thy conservation and preservation, consider, that all thy being dependeth upon the divine providence and disposure, without which, thou canst not move a foot, or subsist the least moment of time. Moreover, for thy use he hath created the whole universal world, and all things therein contained; the earth, the sea, birds, fishes, beasts, plants, nay the very angels themselves he hath ordained to do thee service. Consider thy health, the strength of limbs, and thy very life itself, which thou enjoyest, to be the great benefits of Almighty God, who, by daily nourishment and other temporal helps, conserveth all these in their proper vigor. Observe the miseries and tribulations unto which other mortal men are subject, into which, as others, thou hadst easily fallen, had not the divine goodness protected thee.

In the benefit of thy redemption, consider the abundant good, both in quantity and quality, which he hath purchased to thee by it.

Then call to mind the bitterness of his torments, which he suffered in soul and body to ease thee; and that the acknowledgment of these favors may take a greater impression in thee, in the mystery of his passion take notice of these four things. First, who is it that suffereth; secondly, what he suffered; thirdly, for whom he suffered; fourthly, why he suffered.

He that suffered, was God; what he suffered, were the most grievous torments, and such that never any mortal man did endure the like.

For whom? for most ungrateful creatures, cursed and worthy of hell fire.

Why? not for any commodity or profit of his own, or that we had merited so much by our precedent merits, but only moved to it by his infinite love and bounty towards us.

Concerning the benefit of thy vocation, consider the grace he gave thee, when he infused into thee the Christian faith, by the receiving of baptism and other sacraments, when he did enrol thee in the book of his eternity amongst faithful souls. If, after thy first vocation, when by sin thou hadst lost the innocence of baptism, he hath drawn thee again out of the mire of thy own corruption, restored thee to grace, and brought thee back again into the way of thy own salvation. What thanksgiving oughtest thou to render unto him for so great a benefit? How great was his mercy to thee, that with longanimity he expected so many years; that he permitted thee to spend thy days in so great impurity of wickedness; that he hath often visited thee with good and holy inspirations; that he did not cut off the thread of thy perverse life, as he served others in the same place; to conclude, that he called thee with such efficacious grace, that he restored thee from death to life, and opened thine eyes to contemplate his clear light? How great was his clemency towards thee, that he supported thee with his grace, not to return back again to thy former sins, but to overcome the enemies of mankind, and constantly to persevere in a virtuous cause.

These are the common benefits. Besides these, there are many secret ones, known to none but those that receive them, and others, which, indeed, are not clearly known unto themselves, but only to him that bestowed them. How often for thy pride, arrogance, ingratitude, and sloth, hast thou deserved to be left of God, as many for less causes have been? Yet, notwithstanding, he would not? How often hath God, with his singular providence, exempted thee from evil, removed occasions of offending, broken the snare that the enemy had laid for thy perdition, hath frustrated his expectation, and would not permit that his counsels and machinations should prevail against thee? How often hath he done to us as he did to St. Peter in the gospel: "*Ecce Satanas expetivit vos, ut cribaret sicut triticum: Ego autem rogavi pro te ut non deficiat fides tua:*" "Behold Satan hath desired to have you that he may sift you as wheat, but I have prayed for thee that thy faith fail not."* And who can know these secret benefits but God alone? benefits which are palpable, are easy to be seen, but those which are private, consisting in the working of good, or preventing of ill, the mind of man cannot perfectly comprehend. Wherefore, it is meet and convenient to reason, that we should render immortal thanks to God, for all these benefits, and confess ingenuously, that we have received more than we are able to restore, and that our obligations towards him are so great, that with any goods of ours we shall never live to requite them, when we cannot so much as number or comprehend them in our understanding.

* Luc. c. xxii. v. 31.

CHAPTER III.

OF THE TIME AND FRUIT OF THESE MEDITATIONS.

Behold, Christian reader, thou hast seven former meditations, accommodated to every day of the week; not so that it is an offence to meditate upon another matter; when, as we said before, whatsoever inflameth the heart to the love and fear of God, and to the keeping of his commandments, may profitably be assumed for matter of meditation. We, therefore, out of so great a number, have selected these, both for that they contain the chief mysteries of our faith, and that in them is force and efficacy, to rouse up our souls to the love and fear of God: as also to set before novices, which have need of a guide, prepared and, as it were, fore-chewed matter, lest they confusedly wander up and down in this spacious field, without any certainty, now meditating upon one thing, and presently on another.

The former meditations to whom they properly belong.

Moreover, these meditations, as we have said elsewhere, suit best with those who do begin to turn from Almighty God from their wicked courses. For these had need to be helped by the consideration of these things, to the detestation and horror of sin, the fear of

God, the contempt of the world, which are, as it were, the first steps to the amendment of our former perverse life; therefore, it is good, that they should sometimes insist in them, that they may have the better foundation for other ensuing virtues.

SEVEN OTHER MEDITATIONS

OF

THE PASSION OF OUR LORD,

AND THE MANNER HOW IT OUGHT TO BE MEDITATED UPON.

CHAPTER IV.

HERE follow seven other meditations of the passion of Christ, his resurrection, and ascension into heaven; to which, others of his holy life may well be added.

But we must note, that in the passion of our blessed Saviour, six things chiefly are to be meditated upon. First, the bitterness of his sorrow, that we may compassionate with him. Secondly, the greatness of our sins, which were the cause of his torments, that we may abhor them. Thirdly, the greatness of the benefit, that we may be grateful for it. Fourthly, the excellency of the divine charity and bounty therein manifested, that we may love him more fervently. Fifthly, the conveniency of the mystery, that we may be drawn to admiration of it. Lastly, the multiplicity of virtues of our blessed Saviour which did shine in this stupendous mystery, that we may partly imitate and partly admire them; wherefore, in the midst of these meditations, let us sometimes compassionate with our blessed Saviour in the extremity of his sorrows; extreme indeed, both by reason of the tenderness of his body, as also, for the great affection he bore unto our souls. He did suffer them without any manner of consolation, as we shall speak hereafter in its proper place. Sometimes let us stir up in ourselves compunction for our sins, which were the cause of these his great sufferings. Sometimes let us kindle in our souls an ardent affection, considering his great affection towards us, which upon the cross he declared and manifested to the whole world. And the benefit which he bestowed upon us in his passion, because he bought us with the inestimable price of his precious blood, of which only, we reap the benefit and commodity. Sometimes let us ruminate upon the conveniency of the manner, his eternal wisdom would be pleased to choose, to cure our miseries, to satisfy for our sins. to relieve our necessities, to make us partakers of his glory, to repress our pride, to induce us to the love and joyful suffering of poverty, injuries, austerity, and all commendable laborious exercises. Moreover, it will not be besides the matter, to look into the admirable examples which did principally shine in the life and passion of our sweet Saviour, his meekness, patience, obedience, mercy, poverty, charity, humility, bounty, modesty, and other of his rare virtues, which in all his actions did glitter like stars in the firmament. And chiefly to this end, let us meditate upon these things, that, as near as we can, we may imitate them. Let us shake off sloth, and elevate our souls, that as much as in our power lieth, with the help of his holy grace, we may trace his sacred footsteps. This is the best and most profitable method of meditating upon our blessed Saviour's passion, that is to say, that, thereby we be drawn to imitation, and so to be wholly transformed into our blessed Saviour, that each one may say with the Apostle: "*Vivo autem, jam non ego, vivit vero in me Christus.*" "And now I live, but not I, but Christ in me." Moreover, in meditating our blessed Saviour's passion, we must set him before the eyes of our souls, imagining that we see as present the pangs of his heavy sufferings; and we must not only insist upon the bare history of his passion, but we must consider other circumstances; namely, these four: first, who it is that suffereth? secondly, for whom? thirdly, how? fourthly, why? First, he that suffereth, is God, omnipotent, infinite, immense. For whom? the most ungrateful creature in the world, and less regarding his benefits. How? with most profound humility, charity, bounty, meekness, mercy, patience, modesty, &c. Why? not for his own commodity, nor our merits, but for his immense piety, mercy, goodness and love towards us.

Last of all, let us not only contemplate his outward, but his inward torments, for much more may be considered in the soul than in the body of Christ, both for the more sensible feeling of his passion there, as also for divers other considerations therein. Thus, having set down this short preface, let us proceed to the handling of the mysteries themselves of our blessed Saviour's passion.

SEVEN OTHER MEDITATIONS.

A MEDITATION FOR MONDAY.

This day, after thou hast signed thyself with the sign of the cross, thou shalt meditate upon the washing of the disciples feet, and institution of the blessed sacrament.

Consider, O my soul, at this supper, sweet Jesus himself to be present, contemplate that inestimable example of humility, which he there proposed unto thee for imitation; when rising from the table where he sat with his disciples, he would be pleased to wash their feet. O sweet Jesus, what is it that thou dost? O sweet Jesus, why doth thy mighty Majesty thus diminish itself? O my soul, what wouldst thou have thought to see God kneeling at the feet of men, and prostrate before Judas? O barbarous and cruel man, could not so great humility mollify thy heart? Was not so great bounty and sweetness able to penetrate thy entrails, and to reclaim thee from thy intended mischief? can it be that thou determinest to sell this meek lamb for so small a price? nay, if it be so, how couldst thou yet endure to behold so rare an example? I wonder it did not wound thy guilty soul with compunction for thy grievous crime? O delicate hands, how could you touch so filthy, sordid, and with sin contaminated feet? O pure and unspotted hands, how could you endure to wash those feet, that were stained with going and coming to make a sale of your precious blood? O thrice happy Apostles, did you not tremble and stand amazed at the sight of so great humility? What dost thou do, Peter? canst thou permit the Lord of Majesty to wash thy feet? St. Peter, wholly astonished with the admiration of this spectacle, when he saw our blessed Saviour falling down at his feet, cried out, "*Domine, tu mihi lavas pedes?*" Lord, dost thou wash my feet? what, art not thou the son of the ever-living God? art not thou the creator of the whole world, the beauty of heaven, the paradise of angels, redeemer of mankind, splendor of thy father's glory, most deep fountain of the eternal wisdom? and dost thou wash my feet? how cometh it to pass, that thou Lord of so great majesty and glory, shouldst thus debase thyself to so vile a service?

Then, consider, how he washed all his disciples' feet, one by one, and after washing, wiped them with a linen cloth wherewith he was girded, open the eyes of thy mind to behold in these mysteries, a representation of our redemption. This linen cloth so wiped their feet, that all the dirt which was upon their feet did stick on the linen cloth, not without mystery.

For what more foul than man conceived in sin? What more pure than Christ conceived by the operation of the Holy Ghost? "*Dilectus meus candidus et rubicundus, electus ex milibus.*"* "My beloved," saith the spouse in the canticles "is white, and ruddy chosen out of thousands;" yet, notwithstanding, most pure, most beautiful. Christ took unto himself all the spots of our souls; from which, that he might cleanse us, (as you may see him upon the cross,) he would be pleased to defile himself with the filth of our impurity. Consider, lastly, with what words our blessed Saviour closed up this humble action: "*Exemplum enim dedi vobis ut quemadmodum ego feci vobis, ita, et vos faciatis.*" "For I have given you an example, that as I have done to you, so you do also."† Which words do not only pertain to this present action and example of humility, but likewise to all the actions of Christ throughout his whole life, which is a most absolute and perfect rule for us to square our actions by, especially of humility, which is here to life represented unto us.

* Cant. c. v. v. 10. † John, c. xiii. v. 15.

OF THE INSTITUTION OF THE BLESSED SACRAMENT.

He that desireth to comprehend anything of this noble mystery, must certainly think, that no tongue is able to express that immense love and ardent affection, wherewith our blessed Saviour was inflamed towards his holy church and all faithful souls, in instituting this stupendous mystery. For when this bridegroom determined to depart out of this mortal life, and to leave the church his beloved spouse; lest this his departure should be any occasion to her of forgetting her redeemer; he gave her this sacrament wherein he himself is present, as a pledge and memorial of his perpetual love.

The causes why Christ instituted this Sacrament.

The first.

Then seeing he was to be long absent, lest his spouse should remain solitary alone, he, for his consolation, would leave himself for her companion in this holy sacrament.

The second.

When our blessed Saviour was to suffer death for the redemption of his spouse, to enrich her with his most precious blood, and to purge her from sins, lest she should be defrauded of so great a treasure; he would give her a key in this sacrament whereby she might at her pleasure enjoy these riches; for as St. Chrysostom saith, we

The third.

must think as often as we come to this sacrament, we put our mouth to the bleeding side of Christ, and from thence drink his most precious blood, whose merits we participate.

The fourth. Moreover, this celestial bridegroom, did desire to be tenderly beloved of his spouse, and for this cause would leave her this mystical meat, consecrated with most efficacious words, and therein so great virtue, that whosoever receives it worthily shall presently be struck with the darts of love.

The fifth. He would likewise bestow upon his spouse some pure pledge, thereby to make her secure of the certain succession of future glory, that in hope of so great a good, he might temper the laborious difficulty, and make the tedious bitterness of this present life to be more tolerable; wherefore, that the spouse might certainly believe that she shall at length attain to these unspeakable goods, he hath given her for a pawn, this inestimable treasure, which is as much worth as that which is expected hereafter; that she should not doubt but that God will give her himself in glory, where he liveth in spirit, that would be pleased to give her himself in this vale of tears, where he liveth in the flesh.

The sixth. He would, moreover, when he died, make his last will and testament, wherein he left to his spouse a singular manna, to cure all her infirmities; a gift, than which nothing can be more sovereign, nothing more precious, seeing the Deity itself is therein contained.

Lastly, he desired to feed our souls with some heavenly food, seeing they need no less nourishment than they might live spiritually, than the body needeth corporal sustenance, that she might live corporally. Wherefore, this spiritual physician, when he had diligently examined and felt the pulse of our fragility, instituted this holy sacrament, which he exhibited unto us under the species or form of bread, that he might declare what effect it should work in us, that is to say, that it is as necessary for our souls as bread for the body. *The seventh.*

A MEDITATION FOR TUESDAY.

THIS day thou shalt meditate of the prayer Christ made in the garden, the method thereof; and the contumelies he suffered in the house of Annas.

Consider, therefore, how Christ our Lord, after the consummation of his mystical body with his disciples, before he entered into the tragedy of his passion, went to make his prayer upon the mount Olivet; whereby he would instruct us, that in all adversities and tribulations of this present life, we fly to prayer, as to a holy anchor; the power of which is so great, that it either beateth back the forces of tribulations, or (which is of greater excellency) ministereth sufficient strength to endure them, with a constant and willing mind.

He took, for his companions in his journey, three of his disciples, whom he loved above the rest: St. Peter, St. James, and St. John. Who, as they were eye-witnesses of his transfiguration, so likewise, they should be present in his agony, to behold him, for the love of man, now transformed into a far more different shape than he was when he manifested himself unto them in a glorious and glittering form.

That, also, he might open unto them his inward grief to be much greater than appeared outwardly. He saith unto them: "*Tristis est anima mea usque ad mortem. Sustinete hic, et vigilate mecum:*" "My soul is sorrowful even unto death. Stay you here and watch with me."* O words full of compassion! Then departing from his disciples a stone's cast, with great submission and reverence, he prayed his Father: "*Pater mi, si possible est, transeat a me calix iste, verumtamen non sicut ego volo, sed sicut tu.*" "My Father, if it be possible, let this chalice pass from me. Nevertheless, not as I will, but as thou wilt." Which prayer, when he had repeated thrice, he fell into such an agony that he sweat drops of blood, trickling down upon the earth, from his precious body.

Consider, that partly the foreseeing of the

* Matt. c. xxvi.

most unspeakable torments that ever any mortal man suffered, prepared for his most tender body; partly the distinct representation of the sins of the whole world, for the expiation of which he was now to suffer death upon the cross; partly the remembrance of the ingratitude of many, who would not esteem or reap any profit from this great benefit, struck such a deep impression into his soul, that it filled it with sad and incredible anxiety, so troubled his senses and tender flesh, that all the elements of his body being weakened, the opened pores on every side sweat out drops of blood. If the flesh, which properly suffered not this anguish, but only through a simple imagination, was thus afflicted, what did his soul feel? to whom, properly, these sorrows did appertain.

His prayer being ended, that counterfeit friend of Christ, Judas the traitor, came attended with a hellish band: he, I say, who renounced his apostleship, to be head and captain of a troop of hell-hounds, behold in the fore-front of that wicked multitude, impudently coming to his Master, whom before he had sold, betraying him with a kiss of peace and friendship.

In that hour, said Jesus to the company which came to apprehend him, "Are you come out, as it were against a thief, with swords and clubs? When I was daily with you in the temple, you did not stretch forth your hands against me; but this is your hour, and the power of darkness."*

This mystery is worthy of admiration, for what thing can be more admirable and stupendous, than to see the only begotten Son of God, not only in the form of sinful man, but in the shape of a condemned man: "*Hæc est hora vestra, et potestas tenebrarum:*" "This is your hour, and the power of darkness." From which words is gathered, that this innocent lamb was left to the diabolical cruelty of the princes of darkness, who, by their vicegerents and ministers, poured all the malice and mischief they were able to conceive, against him. Consider how much, for thy sake, the supreme majesty of God is humbled; to endure all the extremity of torments that ever any suffered in this present life, nor to die for his own faults, but for thy sins; but he did undergo this of his own accord, to free thee from the power of Satan.

He had scarce spoken these words, when that whole rabble of hunger-starved wolves, gaping after their prey, rushed upon this meek and innocent lamb, hauling, tearing, and afflicting him, with as much cruelty as ever they could. O barbarous and inhuman proceedings! O cruel and savage blows, contumelious violences, wherewith they tormented him; they insulted after a horrid manner, no otherwise

* Luke, c. xxii. v. 52.

than conquerors return loaded with spoils, after they have put to flight their enemies, or hunters when they have caught their prey. The hands which a little before were exercised in working miracles, they were now bound with ropes so cruelly, that they razed the skin, and besmeared them with blood. Thus they led him through the public streets of Jerusalem, following him with contumelies and blows: behold him in this journey going alone, left by all his disciples, compassed with a multitude of his enemies, forced to make such haste, that he was wholly out of breath, his color changed, his face blushing, and his whole body weakened and wearied by reason of the intolerable present difficulty.

Although our blessed Saviour was barbarously and almost cruelly handled by that blood-sucking multitude, yet, nevertheless, thou mightest have seen in his countenance a pleasant sweetness, in his eyes a comely gravity, in his manners, a divine grace, which all the torments of the whole world could not so much as diminish in the least degree.

After this, go with our blessed Saviour into the house of Annas the high priest, that there thou mayest take notice what favor he reaped for his mild answer, when Annas examined him of his, and his disciples' doctrine, which was, that one of the officers gave him a cruel blow upon his cheek, saying, "*Sic respondes pontefici?*" "Answerest thou the high priest so?" To him Christ replied: "*Si male locutus sum, testimonium perhibe de malo: si autem bene, quid me cædis?*"* "If I have spoken evil, bring testimony of the evil, but if well, why strikest thou me?"

Behold, O my soul, not only the mild answer, but the print of the officer's hand in his tender cheek, his countenance, notwithstanding, quiet and amiable, not a whit moved at the shame of so great an affront, because he inwardly thought so low and humbly of himself, that he had turned the other side without delay, if the rascal had desired it.

A MEDITATION FOR WEDNESDAY.

THIS day thou shalt consider, how Christ our Lord was offered up to Caiphas the high priest; what torments he endured there all that night; how St. Peter denied him; and last of all, how cruelly he was scourged.

Consider, first of all, how he was led from the house of Annas to the house of Caiphas; it is worth thy pains to follow him thither; for there thou shalt see the mighty sun of justice eclipsed; there thou shalt behold that divine face, upon which, the angels themselves delight to gaze, deformed with the filthy spittings of the Jews; for our Blessed Saviour standing in the midst of them, was conjured by the high

* John. c. xviii. v. 23.

priest in the name of his Father, to speak out what he was. He answered as beseeming himself; but they, who were unworthy of such an answer, blinded with the splendor of this great light like mad dogs, rushed upon him, vomiting up the bitter gall of their whole malice against him.

They began, whole troops of them to buffet him, to beat and kick him, they spat upon his divine face, and threw the very filth of their noses upon it. Others hood-winked his eyes with a dirty linen cloth, smiting him upon his cheek, and would in mockery have him prophecy who it was that struck him. O admirable and unheard-of patience, and humility of the only begotten Son of God. Oh, behold that face, which the angels of heaven do contemplate with incredible joy, besmeared with their sordid and filthy spittings.

Men, when they spit, commonly turn themselves to some foul place, somewhat remote from the sight of others. In this palace was there no place found more contemptible therein to cast their spit and filthy drivel, than the sacred face of Jesus Christ? O man, that art but dust and ashes, canst thou choose but be stirred up to humility, and contempt of thyself, at so rare an example?

Consider, moreover, what torments our Blessed Saviour suffered all that night, how the officers that kept him, afflicted him, that sleep should not close his eyes, derided the supreme Majesty of God, and loaded him with many injurious contumelies.

Weigh with thyself, my soul, that now thy spouse is made the white and mark, receiving upon himself all the darts of injurious contumelies that the mischievous Jews could shoot at him. O cruel night, O unquiet night, in which thou Blessed Jesus could rest no more by reason of anguish and affliction, than others who took pleasure to torment thee. The night was ordained for the rest of all creatures, that the members and senses wearied with the labor of the day before, might then take some repose. But the wicked soldiers that kept thee, spent it in tormenting thy senses, they did bind thy body, vexed thy soul, fettered thy hands and feet with manacles, buffetted thy cheeks, spat upon thy face, blinded thine eyes, so that all thy senses, when they should have been refreshed, were afflicted.

Oh! how far did these matins differ from those, which, at the same time, the blessed angels did sing in heaven? they cried holy, holy, and the Jews cried, he is guilty of death, crucify, crucify him. O angelical spirits which understand both cries, what could you imagine or think, when you saw the inhuman cruelty wherewith he was handled on earth, whom in heaven you adored with such great submission and reverence? did you not wonder to see him suffer all these extreme torments, to expiate the sins of those who inflicted them upon him?

who hath ever heard of such immense charity, that for this reason one should suffer death, to heal the grief, and cure the wounds of his murderers?

The fall of St. Peter, that great pillar, did not a little increase the anxiety of this tedious night; that he, whom he entirely loved amongst the rest, whom he chose to present at his glorious transfiguration, to whom he committed the primacy of his holy church, whom he ordained to be head and prince of the Apostles, that he, I say, should before his face, and in his presence, deny him, not once, but thrice, adding blasphemies and oaths, that he knew not the man. Tell me, Peter, did this man seem to thee so ungodly and wicked, that in future times thou didst fear, it would be a disgrace unto thee to confess him now? didst thou not consider that thou didst first pronounce the sentence of condemnation against him, before he was adjudged by the high priests, when thou didst not esteem him so much as worthy of thy acknowledgment? couldst thou do a greater injury to Jesus Christ?

But Christ, sorrowful for this great fault of St. Peter, turned himself, and cast his eyes upon him, that with his gracious countenance, he might reduce this wandering sheep into the sheepfold of his mercies. O admirable aspect, secret indeed, but full of signification, which St. Peter knew right well, and well understood of what force and efficacy it was. The crowing of the cock had little availed to his compunction and conversion, had not the countenance of Christ our Saviour been adjoined; whose eyes did speak and work that stupendous change, the certainty of which, not only the flowing tears of St. Peter, but of our Blessed Saviour himself, did sufficiently testify.

After all these injuries, consider what Christ suffered, when he was bound to be scourged at the pillar, for the judge, when he saw that he could not pacify the fury of those infernal monsters, thought good to advise them, to beat him with rods and whips, whereby his whole body might be torn, hoping that way to mollify their obstinate and obdurate hearts; that when they saw him so torn and mangled, they would cease further to desire his cruel death.

Enter now, my soul, in spirit, into the house of Pilate, and have tears in readiness, for thou wilt have need of them, if thou shalt diligently consider what was done there.

Behold, how inhumanly these abject and infamous rogues despoiled our Blessed Saviour of his garments. Mark the humility of Christ, how he suffered himself to be stripped, not so much as opening his mouth, nor uttering any word against their injurious behaviour. See his sacred body bound to the pillar with many ropes, in such a fashion, that on every side they might have room to torture him.

Consider, how the Lord of angels, stood alone in the midst of his cruel enemies, without any advocates, or procurators, that would defend his cause, yea, altogether without any one man, who, at leastwise, afar off, would so much as compassionate the bitterness of his torments. Dost thou not hear the noise of rods and whips, wherewith they loaded, tore, and rent the delicate flesh of Jesus, adding stroke upon stroke, and wound to wound? dost thou not see his whole body in one short moment of time, with the vehemency, and often reiterated blows, to be covered, as it were, with one ulcer, his skin to be drawn from the flesh, and blood from his whole body, from the crown of his head to the soles of his feet, to flow down upon the earth? especially, is it not dreadful for thee to behold the place between the shoulders, whereupon, almost the whole force of the blows did light?

Consider, how Christ, the Saviour of the world, after that extreme cruelty of his tormentors, went up and down the palace all torn and cut, seeking and gathering up his garments, not finding one amongst those inhuman rascals, that would show unto him the least act of humanity, in washing or refreshing his wounds, or lend their hand to help him to put on his clothes. All these things are worthy of our diligent consideration, that thereby we might stir up our souls to due compassion of his miseries.

A MEDITATION FOR THURSDAY.

This day thou shalt meditate how Christ was crowned with thorns; his presentation before all the people; his condemnation; his bringing out to the place of execution; and, last of all, his carrying of his cross.

The spouse in the Canticles invited us to the consideration of these torments, when she said, "*Egredimini et videte filiæ Sion Regem Salomonem in diademate, quo coronavit illum mater sua in die desponsationis illius, et in die lætitiæ cordis ejus:*"*

"Go forth ye daughters of Sion, and see King Solomon in the diadem wherewith his mother hath crowned him, in the day of his espousals, and in the day of the joy of his heart."

What dost thou do? what dost thou think, my soul? my tongue, why art thou silent? O sweet Saviour, when I open mine eyes and behold this sorrowful spectacle, my heart is rent with grief. What, Lord, were not thy former torments, imminent death, and abundance of thy blood already shed, sufficient for the redemption of mankind? but thou must yet be crowned with sharp thorns?

My soul, that thou mayest the better understand this sad spectacle, set before thine eyes,

* Canticles, c. iii. v. 11.

our Blessed Saviour in his former beauty, before he suffered these torments: then behold him, on the contrary, in this miserable state. If in the first, thou dost rightly view him, thou shalt see him more beautiful than the sun: in his eyes a comely gravity; in his speech a gracious facility; in his actions singular modesty; in the gesture of his whole body profound humility, joined with reverend majesty.

Then, after thou hast satiated thy soul with pleasure, in beholding this rare piece of admirable perfection, then turn thine eyes again, and look upon him as he is, in this present miserable state. Ridiculously clothed in purple, bearing in his hand a reed for a kingly sceptre, and upon his head a crown of sharp thorns, instead of a regal diadem: his eyes were dimmed, his face pale and wan, fouled and covered with the filthy spittle of the Jews; behold him within and without! his heart consumed with grief, his body torn with wounds and blows, forsaken of his disciples, hastened to undergo death from his enemies; mocked of the soldiers, despised of the high-priests, rejected as a wicked king arrogantly assuming this title, unjustly accused, and destitute of all human aid.

Do not consider these things as done and past many years since, but imagine with thyself, that at this present time they are acting before thy face, not as another man's sorrows, but as thine own afflictions: set thyself in his place, and conjecture what torments thou shouldst suffer, if thy head were bored to the skull, and thy brain-pan pierced with sharp thorns? But what do I say, thorns? when thou canst scarce endure the prick of a small needle. How great, then, was the pain his tender head suffered, with this new and unheard-of torment?

The coronation of our Blessed Saviour, with many mocks and scorns, being ended, the judge produced him before the people, saying: "*Ecce Homo*:" "Behold the man." If ye thirst after the death of the man, behold him scarce a hair's-breadth distant from it; yea, he is brought to that pass, that he deserveth rather commisseration than your envy; if ye fear that he will make himself king, behold, he is so deformed, that he scarce retaineth the shape of a man: do ye fear any violence from these hands that are so straightly manacled? do ye dread any harm from a man that is cast into such a miserable and dejected state? whose body is so mangled and weakened?

Consider, O my soul, in what state thy Saviour was, when the very judge himself did think that this aspect would move his bloody enemies to compassion: from which we may gather, what a miserable thing it is to see a Christian of such an obdurate heart, which cannot or will not condole with the sufferings of our Saviour, when they were such, that the very judge did think them sufficient to mollify the malice of his enemies. But Pilate, seeing with these exceeding torments he could no way temper or assuage their fury, went into his palace, and sat in the judgment-seat to pronounce the definitive sentence against Christ. Now the cross was prepared at the door, and the fatal standard which threatened ruin to our Blessed Saviour, was now in readiness.

The sentence being pronounced, with the addition of more torments, they loaded his wearied shoulders with a heavy cross, to carry to the place of his execution.

But our meek Lord not only not rejected it, but out of that immense charity towards us, wherewith he suffered for our sins, obediently and willingly embraced it.

Now the innocent Isaac, with his weak shoulders, supported the intolerable burthen of the cross to the place of sacrifice. The simple people and devout women, followed him weeping. For who was able to contain tears, to see the Lord and King of angels going thus on foot, with the extremity of torments? his knees quivering, his body stooping, his eyes blinded, his face besmeared with blood, his head crowned with thorns, and his ears deafened with the noise of drums and trumpets.

Leave awhile, O my soul, this horrid spectacle, and with watering eyes, with sobs and sighs, go to the Blessed Virgin and say to her: Lady of angels, queen of heaven, gate of paradise, advocate of the world, sanctuary of sinners, health of the just, joy of the saints, mistress of virtue, mirror of purity, symbol of chastity, pattern of patience, and rule of all perfection. O me, miserable and unfortunate, what have I seen with the eyes of faith? How could I live to behold such inhuman usage? interrupting sighs will not permit me scarce to speak how I left thy only begotten Son, loaded with a mighty cross, to which he was presently to be nailed, and carrying it to the place of execution.

What heart, what mind, what soul, is able to comprehend the dolour, the Blessed Virgin Mary then did suffer? her heart fainted, and a dead sweat with extreme anguish possessed her whole body, and presently she had given up the ghost, had not the divine dispensation reserved her till better times, for her greater merit, and more abundant reward.

The Blessed Virgin with speed followed the steps of her beloved Son; that ardent desire wherewith she was inflamed to see him, added vigor to her, of which sorrow had bereft her: she heard afar off the noise of arms, the concourse of people, and the sound of trumpets on every side, publishing the passion of Christ; after that, she saw the glittering of lances and halberts; in the way she found his footsteps sprinkled with drops of blood, by which, without any guide or leader, she might easily find the way. Approaching to her Son, she lifted up her eyes swelled with tears, to behold him whom she esteemed dearer than her own soul.

Oh! what strife was there in the soul of this Blessed Virgin betwixt fear and love? she did vehemently desire to see her Son, but, on the other side, she durst not cast her eyes upon him in this lamentable and afflicted state. At length, when she drew nearer, these two celestial lights beheld each other, their eyes pierced each other's souls, but grief enforced their tongues to silence; notwithstanding, their hearts did mutually discourse, and the Son unto the mother said: sweet mother, why comest thou hither, my love, O my dove? thy sorrow reneweth my miseries, and my torments crucify thy soul! return, return again into thy house; this defiled company of thieves and murderers, beseemeth not thy virginal purity. These and the like words they inwardly uttered all the way until they came to the place of execution.

A MEDITATION FOR FRIDAY.

This day thou shalt meditate upon the mystery of the cross, and the seven words which Christ spoke upon it. Rouse up, my soul, and duly ponder this great mystery of the cross, which brought forth the fruit of satisfaction, to expiate that great loss which all mankind suffered by a tree.

Consider how, before our Blessed Saviour came to the Mount of Calvary, (to make his death more ignominious) his cruel tormentors stripped him of all his clothes, except his coat, which was without seam: behold how patiently this meek lamb suffereth his garments to be taken from him, not so much as opening his mouth or speaking one word against their barbarous dealing. He permitted these things willingly, but with a great strain to modesty. He was stripped naked that we might receive a better garment, to cover the nakedness of our sins, than that which Adam, the first parent of all mankind, made of the leaves of fig-trees, to cover the nakedness of his body.

Some doctors think that the crown of thorns was taken off, to pull with more facility his unseamed garment over his ears, and after to be fastened on again, which could not be without a vehement pain; the sharp thorns did afresh wound his sacred head with unspeakable torment. And surely this is not unlikely, seeing in the whole time of his passion they spared him in nothing; but the bitterest torments they could devise, they heaped upon him, especially when the Evangelist saith, they did to him whatsoever they would. This coat did so cleave to the wounds of his sacred body, by reason of the congealed blood, that when the barbarous hangmen drew it off with exceeding violence, they renewed again the wounds of Jesus; they pulled off with it many particles of flesh, so that the whole body of Christ, in every part flayed and bloody from the head to the foot, seemed to be, but one entire and continuous wound.

Weigh well with thyself, my soul, the immense goodness and mercy of God, manifested in these torments; behold, him that spreadeth the heavens with clouds, vesteth the green and pleasant fields with flowers, and he, that liberally bestoweth clothing upon every creature, behold him, I say, stark naked! Consider what cold, this precious body, being wounded, suffered; when they had not only despoiled him of his garments, but his very skin was not entire, neither were his wounds bound up, but exposed to the injury of the air. If St. Peter, being well clothed, could not overcome the cold of the forepassed night, what cold dost thou think, this delicate body suffered, being in every place wounded, and all naked.

Then, consider, how Christ was fastened to the cross, and what torment he suffered when the sharp nails pierced the most sensible parts of his tender body. Weigh, with thyself, that the Blessed Virgin, who beheld these things with her eyes, and hearing the frequent blows of the mallet, in driving the nails into the hands and feet of her Son, was not insensible, but that the heart of the Mother was pierced, with the hands, and feet of the Son.

When Christ was made fast upon the cross, presently they lifted it up and put it into a hole, there before prepared; behold how these wicked torturers of the innocent Jesus, pricked forward with their own malice, let the heavy cross fall into the hole with such violence, that it so much strained his body, hanging only by the nails, and rent wider the wounds of his hands and feet.

Sweet Saviour, can there be found a heart so hard, and steely, which is not mollified at such a spectacle, when the very stones did cleave asunder, as sensible of thy cruel torments?

O Lord, the dolours of death compassed thee round about; the storms and waves of the raging sea environed thee on every side, the waters entered into thy soul: thou didst descend to the deep abyss, where thou couldst find no footing. When thy heavenly Father did forsake thee, Lord, what couldst thou expect thy enemies would do? they cried out against thee, and thy friends did wound thy heart; thy soul was sad and heavy, neither was there any that would comfort thee.

Lord, from these unheard-of torments, and abundant satisfaction which thou madest for my sins, I cannot but acknowledge, with all humility, the grievousness of my heinous transgressions, which were the occasions of all thy miseries. I see thee, my King and God, fastened upon a wooden cross, with two iron nails; thy precious and tender flesh, to be stretched without any manner of respite. If thou wouldst a little ease thyself upon thy feet, the weight of thy whole body enlargeth their wounds: if thou wouldst leave the burthen to thy hands, the weight of it doth likewise rend their wounds. Thy sacred head could find no rest, because thou hadst no other pillow than the sharp crown of thorns.

O Virgin Mother, how willingly wouldst thou have embraced him in thine arms, thereon to ease and rest himself a little : but the arms of the cross would not permit thee, upon which, if he would repose, the sharp thorns struck deeper into his head. The troubles of the Son were much augmented by the presence of the Mother; which no less crucified his soul, than the Jews, his body, to the cross.

O sweet Jesus, in one day thou didst carry a double cross, the one upon thy body, the other in thy soul; the one of passion, the other of compassion; the one pierced thy body with nails of iron, the other thy soul with nails of sorrow. What tongue is able to express what thou didst suffer to see the anguish of thy dear Mother, whose soul thou didst certainly know to be crucified together with thee, when thou didst behold her heavy heart, pierced with the sword of sorrow? when with bloody eyes thou didst look upon her beautiful face, pale and wan, and didst hear the sighs of her dying soul, lamenting that she could not die? What didst thou suffer to see pure fountains of tears gushing from her eyes, and to hear her pitiful complaints she made in sorrowing for thy sufferings!

Then, consider, the seven words which Christ spoke upon the cross to his heavenly

Father, saying, "*Pater dimitte illis: non enim sciunt quid faciunt.*" "Father forgive them, for they know not what they do." To the thief: "This day thou shalt be with me in paradise." To his Mother: "Woman behold thy Son." To the people he said: "I thirst." And to God again: "My God, my God, why hast thou forsaken me?" "*Consummatum est:*" "It is consummated." Into thy hands I commend my spirit.

Ruminate, my soul, with what exceeding charity, he made intercession to his heavenly Father, for his enemies and persecutors; with what piety and mercy he received the penitent thief into his favor; with what affection he committed his mother to the protection of his beloved disciple; with what ardor he testified himself vehemently to thirst after the salvation of mankind; with what clamor he thundered out his prayer, expressing to the divine Majesty the grievousness of his tribulations; how perfectly he fulfilled the obedience enjoined to him by his heavenly Father; and lastly, how he yielded his soul into his blessed hands.

Every one of which words do afford us a great deal of matter for our instruction; in the first, we are taught to love our enemies; in the second, mercy towards sinners; in the third, piety towards our parents; in the fourth, to thirst after our neighbor's salvation; in the fifth, when we are oppressed with tribulations, and seeming as it were, to be left of God, to fly to prayer; in the sixth, the virtue of obedience and perseverance; in the seventh, perfect resignation into the hands of God, which is the sum of all perfection.

A MEDITATION FOR SATURDAY.

THIS day thou shalt meditate upon the piercing of our Blessed Saviour's side with a spear; the taking down of Christ from the cross: the lamentations of the women; and other things which did occur about his burial.

First, take notice, how that Christ, after he gave up the ghost upon the cross, his enemies much rejoiced at his death. But yet, there was not an end of their insatiate cruelty, but still their increasing malice raged against him, being dead. They divided, and cast lots for his garments, and with a spear pierced his precious side.

O barbarous caitiffs! O adamantine hearts! did you think those torments he suffered before his death were not sufficient, that you would not vouchsafe to spare him being dead? what madness did possess your souls? lift up your eyes and behold his dead face, his eyes sunk, his hanging head, and his whole body being wan and pale. Although your hearts be harder than adamant, yet let this pitiful aspect mollify them.

Behold the centurion struck a lance into his sacred side, with such violence, that the very cross did tremble, out of whose side did gush abundance of blood and water, for the redemption of all mankind. O river of paradise, running forth to water the whole earth! O precious wound which rather the love thou didst bear to us sinful men, than the enemies' weapon did inflict! O gate of heaven, window of paradise, place of rest, tower of fortitude, sanctuary of the just, nest of doves, tomb of pilgrims, flourishing bed of the spouse! Hail, sacred wound, which piercest devout hearts; hail, rose of incredible beauty; hail, precious stone of inestimable valor; hail, door, through which lieth open a free passage to the heart of Christ, an argument of his love, and pledge of eternal felicity!

Consider, that in the evening, Joseph and Nicodemus came with ladders to loose and take down the body of our Saviour; but the Blessed Virgin, after all these torments, perceiving her Son to be taken from the cross, and disposed for the grave, she took him when he was let down, in her arms, humbly beseeching that holy company, that they would suffer her to come near his body, and to bestow her last kiss and embracings upon him, which upon the cross she could not do, (which they would not, nor could deny; for if her friends had deprived her of him dead, which her enemies did her, of him living, they had redoubled the anguish of her soul.

When she saw her Son in this case, what

grief, what dolors can we imagine she then did suffer? angels of peace come and lament with this blessed Virgin, lament heaven, lament stars, lament all creatures of the world. She embraced the mangled body of her Beloved Son, she hugged him in her arms, (for love administered this strength,) she thrust her face amongst the thorns to come to kiss his mouth, whereby she wounded her face with the sharp pricks which she washed with flowing tears.

O sweet Mother, is this thy Beloved Son? is this he whom thou didst conceive with great glory, and bring forth with great joy? is this that bright mirror in which thou wert wont to see thyself? all that were present did likewise mourn, the other Mary's, which were there, mourned, the noblemen lamented, heaven and earth, with all creatures, mourned with the Blessed Virgin.

That holy Evangelist lamented, who often embracing the body of his dear Master, said, O my good Lord and Master, who shall hereafter teach and instruct me? with whom now shall I consult on doubtful occasions? upon whose lap shall I now rest myself? who shall now reveal unto me celestial secrets? what sudden change is this? yesterday I rested upon thy sacred breast, where thou didst communicate to me the joys and glory of everlasting life, and now in recompense of that benefit I I embrace thee dead in my arms? is this that countenance which I beheld glorious and transfigured upon the mount of Thabor? is this that face which I saw brighter and more glittering than the sun?

And that Blessed sinner, St. Mary Magdalen lamented, who often kissing the feet of her Saviour, said, O the true light of mine eyes, the only remedy and solace of my soul. If I sin again, who shall hereafter receive me into favor? who shall defend me from the calumnies of the Pharisees? O how altered are these feet from those I washed with my tears! O beloved of my heart, why do I not die with thee? O life of my soul, how can I say I love thee, when I living, see thee dead before me?

Thus, this blessed company did mourn and lament, watering with abundant tears the body of Jesus. The sepulchre being ready, they spiced his holy body with sweet spices, they wrapped it up in a fine linen cloth, bound his head with a handkerchief, laid it upon a bier, carried it to the place of burial, and put it into a new monument.

The monument was covered with a stone, and the face of Mary obscured with a cloud of sorrow. When there again she bade her Son adieu, she then began to be more and more sensible of her solitude; for, then she saw herself to be deprived of the greatest good. But her heart remained buried with her treasure in the grave.

A MEDITATION FOR SUNDAY.

This day thou shalt consider and meditate of the descent of Christ to *Lymbus Patrum*: his resurrection; divers apparitions to the Blessed Virgin Mary; St. Mary Magdalen, and his other disciples; and last of all, his glorious ascension into heaven.

Take notice, therefore, of the incredible joy, the Fathers, which were detained in *Lymbus*, felt at their coming of the Redeemer, who came to free them from the dark prison, wherein they were shut for many thousand years. What prayers, what giving of thanks, did they render to him, who had brought them to the long desired haven of their salvation? they, who return from the East Indies, are wont to say, that they think all their forepassed labors well bestowed, only for that joy they find, the first day of their arrival into their country. If the banishment of a year or two, and the tediousness of a little troublesome journey, can breed such joy in men, what will the absence of three or four thousand years do from that pleasant and celestial country! What joy, therefore, do we think those holy Fathers had, when they took possession of it?

Then, consider, the excessive joy of the Blessed Virgin, when she saw her Son risen from death, when it is most certain, and undoubted, that she felt the greatest sorrow, and affliction, at the ignominious death and passion that could be, her joy must needs excel the rest, in his triumphant resurrection. How great dost thou think was her content and pleasure to see her Son, whom she grievously lamented before his death, living glorious, and attended with a joyful troop of holy patriarchs, whom he brought along with him? What said she? what did she? with what kisses did she salute him? with what affection did she embrace him? what pleasant rivers of tears distilled from her eyes? how earnestly did she desire to follow her Son, had it been permitted to her?

Moreover, take notice, of the joy of the holy Mary's, particularly of her who stood weeping, at the sepulchre of Christ, when, without doubt, she saw him whom her soul loved, she cast herself at his feet when she beheld him living, whom she sought amongst the dead.

After his Mother, he, therefore, appeared to her, who loved him most ardently, and, above others, sought him most diligently and perseverantly, to instruct us, that when we look for God, we must seek him with tears and diligence.

Consider, that after this, he appeared to his disciples going to Emmaus, in the habit of a pilgrim; behold, how courteously he joined himself a companion to them; how familiarly he conversed with them; how handsomely he dissembled his person; and after, with what affection he manifested himself unto them;

and last of all, how he left their tongues, and lips, filled with the delightful discourse of his Majesty. Let thy discourse and talk, be like these disciples, as they travelled in the way, of the love and passion of our Blessed Saviour; and, I dare be bold to say, that he will not deny unto thee his sacred presence.

In the mystery of our Blessed Saviour's ascension, first, consider, that he deferred it for forty days, that in the mean time, often appearing to his disciples, he might instruct them, and with them discourse of the kingdom of heaven; for he would not forsake them by ascending into heaven, before he had disposed their minds to ascend with him spiritually.

Hence we may note, that those are often deprived of the corporal presence of Christ, and of sensible devotion, who, with the wings of contemplation, fly up to heaven and fear no danger. Wherein the divine providence, wherewith it curbeth and governeth the elect, doth wonderfully manifest itself, how it strengtheneth the weak, exerciseth the strong, giveth milk to little ones, prepareth stronger meat for great ones, comforteth some, afflicteth others, and to conclude, accommodates himself to all, according to their several degrees in their spiritual profit. Wherefore, he that is roborated by divine comfort, ought, therefore, not to presume of himself, seeing this sensible consolation is but the meat for infirm ones, and a great sign of weakness; nor he that is exercised by affliction, ought, therefore, to be dejected, seeing temptation is for the most part a testimony of a valiant mind.

Christ ascended up to heaven in the presence of his disciples, that they might be witnesses of this mystery, of which, they were beholders, none can give better testimony to Almighty God's deeds, than he who hath learned them by experience; wherefore, he that would certainly know how good, how sweet, and merciful he is towards his, and what is the force and efficacy of his divine grace, love, providence, and spiritual consolations; let him ask those, who, indeed, have had experience of them, for they, and only they, will give him the best instructions and satisfaction.

Moreover, Christ would ascend, his disciples looking upon him, that they might pursue him with their eyes and spirit, that they might have a cordial feeling of his departure; that in his absence they might fear to remain alone, and that they might the better dispose themselves to receive his holy grace. The prophet Eliseus, when Elias was to be taken and separated from him, desired that he would give his spirit. Elias made answer: "*Rem difficilem postulasti attamen si videris me, quando tollar a te, erit tibi quod petisti: si autem non videris, non erit.*" "Thou hast asked a hard thing; nevertheless, if thou see me when I am taken from thee, thou shalt have what thou hast asked; but if thou see me not, thou shalt not have it."*

In like manner, they shall be heirs of the spirit of Christ, whom love doth cause to mourn for his departure; to whom his absence doth seem grievous, who earnestly, whilst they live in this banishment, desire his holy presence. Such a saint was he that said, thou art gone, my comforter, without any care of me, at thy departure thou didst bless thine, and I saw it not; the angels promised that thou shouldst return again, and I heard them not. Who is able to express or understand, the solitude, trouble, cries, and tears of the Blessed Virgin, of his beloved disciple, St. Mary Magdalen, and the other Apostles, when they saw Christ to be taken from them, who, together with him, carried up their affectionate hearts? and yet, notwithstanding, it is said of them, that they returned with great joy into Jerusalem; the same love and affection which made them bewail the visible loss of their beloved Lord and Master, did likewise cause, that they congratulated each other; much rejoicing at his glory, for it is the nature of true love, not so much to seek the commodity of itself, as the honor and commodity of the person that is beloved.

Last of all, to close up this meditation, it is left to us to consider, with what glory, with what joy, this noble conqueror was brought

* 4 Reg. c. ii. v. 10.

into that heavenly city; what solemnities were then instituted in the glorious paradise, how magnificently was he entertained by those celestial citizens? what a delightful spectacle was it, to see men accompanied with angels, to go in procession, and to sit upon those seats, which for many thousand years were vacant. But a most ravishing joy it was, to behold the sacred humanity of Jesus Christ, for transcending all others, to sit at the right hand of his eternal Father.

All these things are worthy of thy attentive consideration, that thou mayest learn, that the labors thou dost undergo for the love of God, are not spent in vain, therefore, he that humbled himself under all creatures, it was requisite that he should be exalted above all, that the lovers of true glory may trace this path, they must expect if they desire to be above all, that first they be subject to all, even their inferiors.

CHAPTER V.

OF SIX THINGS NECESSARY TO PRAYER.

THESE are the exercises and meditations, Christian reader, wherewith, every day, thou mayest feed thy soul, which if thou dost rightly use, thou wilt never want matter to busy thy mind devoutly. But thou must note, that meditation, if it be well performed, ought to consist of six parts; some of which, go before, others follow, mental prayer.

Six parts necessary for meditation.

First, before we apply ourselves to meditation, it is necessary, that our mind and soul be diligently prepared to this holy exercise; as these strings of an instrument, except they be before-hand well-tuned, will never make a pleasant melody.

Preparation.

After preparation, ought to follow the reading of some holy mystery, according to the distribution of days in the week, which in young beginners is chiefly necessary, until with continual use and custom, matter of meditation offereth itself unto their memories. Then insist upon the matter to be meditated upon.

Reading.

Meditation.

To meditation we must join devout and sincere

Giving of thanks. giving of thanks to God for all his benefits; then a general oblation of *Oblation.* all the life of Christ for recompense of any benefit, and our own works to the honor and glory of God. Last of all, pe- *Petition.* tition, which is chiefly called prayer, wherein we desire all things necessary for our own salvation, of our neighbors, and the good of the whole church.

These six parts, are required to mental prayer, which besides other commodities, they minister abundant matter for meditation, seeing they set before us divers sorts of meats, that if one will not relish our spiritual taste, we may fall upon another; if we be deficient in one, in another we may employ our minds, and kindle our devotion.

But in every meditation, neither all these parts nor order, is always necessary, although, as I said before, to young beginners it is, that they should have a certain method, according to which, they are to guide themselves; wherefore, in that which hath, or shall be said, my intention is not to set down a general rule, or immutable perpetual laws, the violating of which should be a fault; but my meaning is, to introduce, and bring in young beginners and novices into the right way, and method, of meditation; which, when they are once in use, experience, but especially, the Holy Ghost, will better inform them.

CHAPTER VI.

OF THE PREPARATION NECESSARY TO PRAYER.

IT will not be beside our purpose to handle all these parts severally; we will, therefore, first begin with preparation, which we did put first.

He, therefore, who goeth about to meditate, after he hath placed his body after a decent manner, either kneeling or standing, or composing himself in manner of a cross, or prostrating himself upon the ground, or sitting, if infirmity or necessity doth so require, let him first sign himself with the sign of the cross; then let him recollect the dispersed powers of his soul, especially the imagination, and sequester it from all temporal and transitory things. Let him elevate his understanding to God, considering his divine presence, with what due reverence and attention as is requisite; and let him imagine Almighty God himself to be present in his soul, as in very deed he is.

If it be the morning meditation, after a general act of contrition for his sins, let him make to God a general confession; if in the evening, let him examine his conscience concerning all his thoughts, words, and works of that day; of the forgetfulness of the benefits of Almighty

God; and of the sins of his former life; humbly prostrating himself in the sight of the Divine Majesty, in whose presence he now is, after a particular manner, saying the words of the patriarch Abraham: "*Loquor ad Dominum meum, cum sim pulvis et cinis*:" "I will speak to my Lord, seeing I am but dust and ashes."* And singing the psalm:† "To thee have I lifted up my eyes, who dwellest in the heavens. Behold, as the eyes of servants are on the hands of their masters; as the eyes of the handmaid are on the hands of her mistress: so are our eyes unto our Lord God, until he have mercy on us. Have mercy on us, O Lord, have mercy on us. Glory be to the Father," &c.

And because we are not able of ourselves to think any good, but all our sufficiency is from God; and because none can say Lord Jesus, that is to say, call upon the name of Jesus, without the Holy Ghost,‡ to thee, therefore, O Holy Ghost, do I turn myself, with tears imploring thy assistance: "Come, Holy Ghost, send forth from heaven the glittering beams of true light; come, father of the poor; come, giver of rewards; come, light of our hearts, sweet comforter, sweet guest of the soul, sweet refreshing, rest in labor, temperature in heat, in mourning a grateful solace, O blessed light, replenish the hearts of the faithful." Then

* Gen. 18. † Psalm 122. ‡ Cor. 2:

followeth the prayer, *Deus qui corda fidelium, etc.* These being said, he shall pray to God to bestow upon him his divine grace, to assist at this holy exercise, with that attention, due recollection, fear and reverence, beseeming so great a majesty, humbly beseeching him, so to pass over this time of holy prayer, that he may return from thence fortified with new fervor, to execute whatsoever shall belong to his holy service; for prayer which beareth not this fruit is luke-warm, imperfect, and of no moment before God.

CHAPTER VII.

OF READING.

After a due preparation, followeth reading those things that are to be meditated upon; that must not be too hasty, but mature, serious, and quiet; to which the understanding must not only be attentive, to understand those things which are read, but also, and chiefly, the will; that those things which are understood, may give a spiritual gust and feeling. When he falleth upon any place which much moveth his affection, let him there pause awhile, that in his heart it may cause a greater impression. He must also beware not to spend too much time in reading, thereby to hinder meditation, it being a more fruitful exercise; for as much, as things attentively considered, pierce more inwardly and produce greater effect. If, peradventure, sometime it happeneth that the mind be so dispersed, that it cannot settle itself to prayer, then it is better to insist awhile longer in reading, or to join reading to meditation; or after the reading of one point, to pause upon that awhile, then after the same manner to proceed to the others: although the understanding tied to certain words which are read,

What to do when the mind is distracted.

cannot so freely be carried into divers affections, as when it is free from this bond.

In putting out of unprofitable thoughts, violence is to be used.

It is oftentimes very profitable for a man to use some violence to himself, to expel his vain and trifling fancies; after the example of the patriarch Jacob, manfully to wrestle against them, persevering unto the end: after which fight, the victory being obtained, God doth, for the most part, give greater devotion, or more pure contemplation, or some other supernatural gift, which he never denieth to those who faithfully fight in his cause.

CHAPTER VIII.

OF MEDITATION.

After reading, followeth meditation, which is sometimes of such things as can be represented to our imagination; as the life and passion of our Blessed Saviour; the latter-judgment; hell; and the kingdom of heaven. Sometimes of such things as are subject rather to the understanding than imagination; as the consideration of Almighty God's benefits, his bounty, clemency, and other perfections which are in God.

These meditations are called, the one intellectual, the other imaginary. Both which, in these exercises, are to be used after a different manner, as occasion requireth. When the meditation is imaginary, so that the thing meditated upon hath, or ever had, any actual existence or being, we must so frame and represent it to our fancy, as though we were present in the same place, and saw with our eyes those things which were there done. This representation will make the consideration of these things more vivacious, and cause a greater impression in our souls; for if our imagination can comprehend whole cities and countries, with less difficulty can it comprehend one mystery. This helpeth much to the recollection of the mind; this will retain the same busied in itself, as a bee in a hive, where she worketh and disposeth all things diligently. But in these things a moderation must be used; for to run with a violent imagination to Jerusalem, to frame to the fancy those things which are to be meditated there, doth oftentimes hurt the head. Wherefore, it is good to abstain from immoderate imaginations, lest nature, oppressed with too violent apprehensions, becomes infirm and weak.

CHAPTER IX.

OF GIVING OF THANKS.

After meditation, followeth giving of thanks, the occasion of which, must be taken from the matter meditated upon; for example, if the meditation be of the passion of our Saviour, we must give thanks unto him, that, he hath redeemed us from so great torments. If of sins, that with longanimity he hath expected us to do penance. If of the miseries of this life, that he hath preserved us from the greatest part of them. If of death, that hitherto, he hath defended us from the perils of sudden death, and hath favorably granted us time of penance. If of the glory of paradise, that he hath created us to that end; that after the storms and troubles of this present life, we should enjoy eternal felicity; after this manner, we are to proceed in other meditations.

To these benefits, we may join the others which we handled before, to wit, the benefits of our creation, conservation, redemption, and vocation. As much as in us lieth, let us give him thanks, that he hath created us, after his own image and likeness, that he hath given us a memory to remember him, an understanding to know him, and a will to love him, that he hath committed us to the custody of angels, that by the help of our angel guardian, he hath exempted us from many dangers, preserved us from many mortal sins, defended us from death, and malice of the devil, while we were in this case, (which was no less than to free us from everlasting death, to which, by sin, we were obnoxious.) That he would vouchsafe to assume our nature upon him, and for our sakes suffer a most ignominious death; that we were born of Christian parents; that we were regenerated by baptism; that in this present life, he hath promised grace, and unspeakable glory in the world to come; that he hath adopted us for his sons; that in the sacrament of confirmation, he hath fortified us with strong weapons, to fight against the world, the flesh, and the devil; that he hath given himself to us in the sacrament of the altar; that he hath left unto us the sacrament of penance, to recover the grace which was lost by mortal sin; that he hath visited us daily with good and holy inspirations; that he hath given us grace to persevere in holy and pious exercises.

After the same method, we must proceed in accounting other of Almighty God's benefits, as well general as particular, and for all, public or private, manifest or secret, give him thanks; and we must invite all creatures, celestial and terrestrial, to bear us company in this holy exercise, singing the song of the three children: "*Benedicte omnia opera Do-*

mini Domino: laudate et superexaltate eum in sæcula, &c."* And the Psalm:† "*Benedic anima mea Domino: et omnia quæ intra me sunt, nomini sancto ejus. Benedic anima mea Domino: et noli oblivisci omnes retributiones ejus. Qui propitiatur omnibus iniquitatibus tuis: qui sanat omnes infirmitates tuas. Qui redimit de interitu vitam tuam: qui coronat te in misericordia et miserationibus.*" "Bless the Lord, O my soul: and let all that is within me bless his holy name. Bless the Lord, O my soul, and never forget all that he hath done for thee. Who forgiveth all thy iniquities; who healeth all thy diseases. Who redeemeth thy life from destruction, who crowneth thee with mercy and compassion."

* Dan. c. iii. v. 57. † Psal. 102.

CHAPTER X.

OF OBLATION.

CORDIAL thanks being given to God, presently the heart breaketh naturally into that affection, which the kingly prophet David felt in himself, when he said: "*Quid retribuam Domino, pro omnibus quæ retribuit mihi?*"* "What shall I render to our Lord, for all things that he hath rendered to me?" Which desire, we shall in some sort satisfy, if we offer to God whatsoever we have. First, therefore, we must offer to God ourselves, for his perpetual servants, wholly resigning ourselves to his holy will, howsoever he shall please to dispose of us. We must likewise direct all our thoughts, words, and works, whatsoever we shall do or suffer, to the supreme honor and glory of his sacred name. Then we must offer to God the Father, all the merits of his only begotten Son, all the labors and sorrows he did undergo, in this miserable world, to fulfil the will of his heavenly Father, beginning from his nativity, and hard manger, to his contumelious crucifying, and giving up the ghost; forasmuch, as these are all the goods and means,

* Psal. 115.

whereof in the New Testament, he hath left us heirs; wherefore, as that is no less our own, which is given us freely, than that we get with our industry; so the merits of Christ, which he hath freely bestowed upon us, are no less our own, than if we had got them with our sweat and labor.

Hence every man may offer this sacred oblation, as the first, numbering one by one, all the labors and virtues of the life of Christ, his obedience, patience, humility, charity, and his other virtues, seeing these are the most excellent of all oblations, that we can offer to God.

CHAPTER XI.

OF PETITION.

THIS noble oblation being well performed, we may securely and confidently proceed to the asking of any gifts and graces. First, therefore, Almighty God is to be prayed unto, with inflamed charity and ardent zeal of his divine honor, for the conversion of all nations, that all people may be illuminated with the knowledge of him, praying and adoring him as the only true and living God. To this end, from the bottom of our hearts, we may utter the words of the kingly prophet: "*Confiteantur tibi populi Deus: confiteantur tibi populi omnes.*"* "Let people, O God, confess to thee; let all people give praise to thee."

Then, we must pray to God for the prelates of the church, the supreme pastor, cardinals, archbishops, bishops, and other prelates, that he would be pleased so to govern and illuminate them, with the light of his heavenly grace, that they may be able to bring all men to the knowledge and obedience of their Creator.

We must also pray to God for kings and princes, (as St. Paul admonisheth,) and for all

* Psal. 66.

men placed in dignity, that by their diligent care, their subjects may live a quiet life, well instructed with honest manners, for this is grateful to God, that willeth all should be saved, and come to the knowledge of his truth.

Then for all the members of his mystical body ; for the just, that he would be pleased to conserve them in their sanctity ; for sinners, to convert them from their wicked courses, to the amendment of their lives; for the dead, that he would free them from the expiating torments wherein they are detained, and bring them to their eternal rest.

We must pray to God, for the poor infirm captives, bond-slaves or others, in whatsoever tribulation ; that for the merits of his dear Son, he would vouchsafe to help, and free them from all their miseries.

After we have prayed for the good of our neighbors, let us, at length, intreat for our own necessities, which discretion will teach every one in particular (if he be not altogether ignorant of himself,) what they are. But, that we may set down a method for beginners, we will lead them into this pathway. First, therefore, we must pray to God, that through the merits and passion of his only begotten Son, he would pardon our sins, give us grace to avoid them, and to expiate them with good works worthy of penance ; but especially, to implore for help and assistance, against those evil inclinations, and vices, in which we are most addicted, lay-ing open to our heavenly physician, all the wounds of our diseased souls, that with the ointment of holy grace he would heal them.

Then, let us ask, for the most excellent virtues wherein the whole perfection of a Christian man consisteth; for example, faith, hope, charity, fear, humility, patience, obedience, fortitude in adversity, poverty of spirit, contempt of the world, true discretion, purity of intention, and other like to these, which are placed in the supreme top of a spiritual building. Faith, is the prime root and foundation of a Christian; hope, is a staff to defend us from all tribulations of this present life; charity, the end of all perfection; fear of God, the beginning of true wisdom; humility, is the basis and ground work of all virtues; patience, is the strongest armor against the fury of our enemies; obedience, is the most grateful oblation to God, wherein man offereth himself for a sacrifice; discretion, is the eye of the soul; fortitude, the hand thereof, wherewith it bringeth all works unto perfection; purity of intention, directeth all her actions unto God. We must after pray for other virtues, which may help us forward in the way of perfection; as sobriety in meat and drink, moderation of the tongue, custody of the senses, modesty and composition of the outward man, sweetness in giving good example to our neighbors, rigor and severity towards ourselves, and the like.

Last of all, we must conclude this petition,

with a fervent imploring of the divine love, and here to pause awhile, so that the chiefest part of time be spent in an earnest desiring of this grace and favor, seeing in the divine love all our felicity doth consist, to that end, this prayer following will not be unprofitable.

A PRAYER FOR OBTAINING DIVINE LOVE.

GRANT, I beseech thee, O Lord, that I may love thee with all my soul, with all my heart, with all my strength; O my only hope, my perfect glory, my refuge and solace; O my dearest of all friends, sweet spouse, flourishing spouse, sweeter than any honey, delight of my heart, life of my soul, joy of my spirit; O bright day of eternity, clear light of my bowels, paradise of my heart, original of all my good; O my chiefest strength, prepare, O Lord in my soul a delicious bed, that according to thy promise, there thou mayest dwell, and make thy mansion. Mortify in me whatsoever is displeasing to thee, and make me a man according to thine own heart. Pierce the marrow of my soul, wound my heart with the darts of dear affection, and inebriate me with the wine of love.

When shall I perfectly please thee in all things? when shall I cast from me all things contrary to thee? when shall I be wholly thine? when shall I leave to be my own? when shall nothing live in me, but what is thine? when shall I embrace thee with ardent affection? when wilt thou inflame, and consume me with the flames of love? when wilt thou pierce and replenish me on every side with thy sweetness? when wilt thou lay open and manifest to my poverty, that precious kingdom which is within me, that is to say, thy sacred self, with all thy riches? when wilt thou unite me perfectly unto thee? when wilt thou transform and swallow me up wholly in thee, that from thee I may never depart? when wilt thou remove from me all obstacles, which hinder me, that am not one spirit with thee. O beloved of my soul! O delight of my heart! look down upon me and hear me, not for my own merits, but out of thine infinite goodness, instruct, illuminate, direct, and help me in all, and through all, that I neither speak or do any thing, but that which I shall know to be grateful before thy sight.

O my God, my love, my joy, my pleasure, my fortress, and my life! why dost thou not help the poor and needy, imploring thy assistance? thou who fillest heaven and earth, why dost thou suffer my heart to be empty? thou who cloathest the flowers and lilies of the fields with beauty; thou who nourishest the birds of the air; thou who sustainest the least creature of the earth; why art thou unmindful of me, that forgetteth all things for the love of thee? O immense goodness! I had knowledge of thee too late, that I loved thee no sooner. O new and ancient beauty! O miserable was my state, when I lived without thy love! O wretched was my condition, when I knew thee not! O intolerable blindness of my heart, when I saw thee not! I sought thee far abroad, when thou wert within me; yet, at length, though late, I have found thee, let not thy mercy suffer me, O Lord, that ever I forsake or leave thee again.

And, because to have eyes to see thee is one of the chiefest things that pleaseth thee; Lord, give me the eyes of a solitary turtle, to contemplate thee, give me chaste eyes full of modesty, humble and amorous, sanctified and weeping, attentive and discreet eyes, which may understand and perform thy will; Lord, give me grace to behold thee with such eyes, as thou mayest look upon me again, as thou didst upon Peter, when he denied thee, and didst move him to bitter compunction for his sins. Look upon me as thou didst upon the prodigal child, when thou didst run to embrace and kiss him; or as upon the publican, not daring to lift up his eyes to heaven. Behold me with those eyes, that thou didst invite Mary Magdalen to penance, and to wash thy feet with tears; or, with those eyes wherewith the spouse in the Canticles incited thee to her love, when thou saidst: "*Quam pulchra es amica mea, quam pulchra es! occuli tui columbarum.*"*

* Cant. c. iv. v. 1.

"How beautiful art thou, my love, how beautiful art thou! thy eyes are dove's eyes."

That my aspect be pleasing, and that the beauty of my soul be grateful unto thee: do thou, I beseech thee, bestow the gift of virtues and graces upon me, to deck and trim myself, whereby I may live to glorify thy holy name for ever and ever.

O merciful and holy Trinity! Father, Son, and Holy Ghost, one only true God, teach, direct, and help me in all. O Father omnipotent, I beseech thee, by the greatness of thy immense power, to confirm and strengthen my memory in thee only, and to replenish it with holy and pious cogitations. O Son most wise, illuminate my small understanding, with thy eternal wisdom, to know thy everlasting truth, and my own misery. O Holy Ghost, love of the Father and the Son, with thy incomprehensible goodness, make my will conformable to thy divine pleasure, inflame it with such a fire of thy holy love, that no waters which arise from the turbulent fear of evil suggestions, may be able to extinguish it. O holy Trinity and one God; I would to God I could do nothing else but praise and love thee, and as much as all thy holy saints; I would to God I had the love of all creatures in me alone; I would, with a willing mind, transfer and turn it to the love of thee, although this were nothing, in respect of what thou deservest. Only thou thyself canst worthily love and praise thyself, because none else besides thee is able to understand thy incomprehensible goodness, and therefore the just poise of love resideth only in thy sacred breast.

O Blessed Virgin Mary, Mother of God, Queen of heaven, lady of the world, mansion of the Holy Ghost, lily of purity, rose of patience, paradise of pleasure, mirror of chastity, vessel of innocence: intercede for me, miserable banished wretch, and bestow upon me a portion of thy abundant charity.

O all ye saints of God, and ye angelical spirits, who burn with a vehement affection of your Creator, especially ye seraphims, who inflame both heaven and earth with love, do not forsake my miserable soul, but purify it as you did the lips of Isaiah from all vice and uncleanness, and set it on fire with the flames of your ardent love, that I may love and seek our Lord God, resting and remaining in him for ever and ever. Amen.

CHAPTER XII.

CERTAIN DOCUMENTS TO BE OBSERVED ABOUT MEDITATION.

Hitherto we have only set down plentiful matter for meditation, which, for the present, is very necessary, because the greatest part of men either neglect or disdain this exercise, because they want sufficient matter to consider upon; now we will briefly handle those things which pertain to the form and method of meditation, of which, through the Holy Ghost be the principal master, nevertheless, experience teacheth us that certain documents are likewise necessary: because the way to heaven is cragged, and full of difficulties, therefore, is there need of a guide, without which, many have gone astray a long time from the right path, or, at leastwise, have not attained to their desired end so soon as they expected.

THE FIRST DOCUMENT.

The first document therefore, is, that we do not so adhere to those things, which above we have digested into several points and times, as that we should think it a fault to fall upon other things, wherein the mind may reap more abundant fruit; for seeing devotion is the end of all those exercises, that which cometh nearest to this scope is always to be accounted best; which ought not lightly, upon every occasion, to be done, but with a clear and manifest profit.

THE SECOND DOCUMENT.

WE must be wary of too many speculations in this exercise, and use rather efficacious affections of the will, than curious discourses of the understanding: wherefore, they go not in the right way, that meditate of divine mysteries as though they were to preach them to the people in a sermon; which is rather to dissipate, than to recollect the spirit, and to wander abroad, than to be busied in their own home. Therefore, he that will meditate with fruit to his soul, must come to it like an humble simple creature, bringing rather a will disposed to taste these holy mysteries profitably, than acrimony of understanding to discuss them learnedly: for this is proper to those who give themselves to study, not to those who consecrate themselves unto devotion.

THE THIRD DOCUMENT.

IN the preceding document, we declared how the understanding is to be moderated and subjected to the will; now, we will prefix some limits to the will, out of which she cannot deviate without a fault. That, therefore, she be not too immoderate in her exercise, we must know that devotion is never to be expressed with the violence of our arms, as some do think, who with constrained sorrow, do wring out tears and commiseration, while they consider the torments of Jesus Christ; for this doth rather dry the heart, than make it capable of divine visitations (as Cassianus doth excellently teach): moreover, this extraordinary force doth often hurt the body, and by reason of the burthen which this violence bringeth with it, the mind is left so nauseous, that it feareth to return again to these exercises. When experience teacheth that it is the cause of so much trouble, he, therefore, that will fruitfully meditate upon the passion of Christ, let him not be too anxious for sensible commiseration, but let it suffice that he exhibiteth himself present to his sufferings, beholding them with a simple and quiet eye, and considering them with a tender compassionate heart, rather disposed to entertain that affection which Almighty God's mercy shall suggest, than that which shall be wrung out with violence; which, when he hath done, let him not be solicitous nor sorrowful what other things God doth deny or will not give.

THE FOURTH DOCUMENT.

Hence we may gather what attention is to be observed in prayer; wherefore, the heart must not be languishing, remiss, or dejected; but quick, attentive, and elevated to heavenly things. And as it is necessary to come to God with such attention, elevation of the mind, and abstraction from sensible things, so it is no less necessary to temper sweetly this attention, that it be neither hurtful to bodily health, nor impediment to extinguish devotion. For when any be so intensive to the matter they meditate upon, without any respect to their infirm nature, do oftentimes so dull their brains, that they be unapt for other exercises; on the contrary, there are some, to avoid this danger, are so remiss and lazy in their attention, that easily they suffer their minds to be distracted with other idle thoughts.

These two extremes, that they may be both avoided, such moderation is necessary, that the head be not weakened with too violent attention, nor the thoughts permitted carelessly to wander out of supine negligence; in which thing, we must imitate a good rider upon an untoward horse, who neither holdeth him in too hard, nor looseth the reins upon his neck, but guideth him equally, that he giveth not back, nor goeth forward too speedily. So we must strive in meditation, that attention be moderate, diligently resisting evil thoughts, but not violent with anxiety.

We must note also, that these things we here speak of, attention, are chiefly to be taken heed of in the beginning of meditation; for it often happeneth, that those who are too violent in the beginning, do founder in the midst of meditation: as travellers making too much speed in their setting forth, are tired in the midst of their journey.

THE FIFTH DOCUMENT.

Amongst all documents this is chiefly to be observed, that when in meditation we cannot presently perceive that sweetness of devotion we expect, not, therefore, to wax pusillanimous, or leave off from the exercise begun, but patiently, with longanimity, expect the coming of our Lord: seeing it beseemeth the excellency of the Divine Majesty, the utility and baseness of man's condition, the importance of the business we have in hand, to stay awhile before the gates of his sacred palace. If he cometh presently, after a little expectation, with many thanks, let us with gratitude entertain this undeserved favor: if he maketh longer delays, let us humble ourselves before him, and confess that we do not deserve this grace: if he vouchsafest not to come at all, let us bear it patiently with a quiet mind, and content ourselves, that we have offered ourselves, with all we have, unto him, for a grateful sacrifice; that we have denied our own proper wills, resigning them unto his power; that we have crucified all our inordinate appetites; that we have fought against our passions and vices; and, finally, that we have performed whatsoever was in our power to be done; and although we have not worshipped him with sensible devotion, yet let it suffice us, that we have worshipped him in spirit, and in truth, as he requireth.

Last of all, let us persuade ourselves that this is the most dangerous, and chiefly to be feared rock of this present navigation, and place wherein the true and faithful servants of God are tried, and distinguished from infidels; from which, if we shall depart in safety, in all others we shall have a prosperous success.

THE SIXTH DOCUMENT.

This document not much differeth from the former, which, notwithstanding, is equally necessary: and this it is, that the servant of God must not content himself that he hath felt a little sensible gust from meditation, as many do when they have shed a little dry tear, or felt a little mollifying of the heart, that they have attained to the scope and end of this exercise. But they are far deceived; for even as to make the earth fruitful, one little shower which layeth the dust, is not sufficient, but it must have a great deal of rain, thoroughly soaked into the roots of the plants, before it can give any hopes of a fruitful year, so the abundance of celestial waters are necessary to our souls, for to make them bring forth the fruit of good works.

Wherefore, we are not without cause admonished by spiritual men, that we should spend as much time as possibly we can in this holy exercise, and it is better to insist some long time together, than by fits, for when the time is short, it will be almost all consumed in quieting the imagination, and recollecting the heart, and it often happeneth, that whilst we should reap the fruit of our former trouble, meditation is quite broken off.

Concerning the prefixed time for meditation, it seemeth to me, whatsoever is less than two hours, or an hour and a half, is too little for this exercise; because almost one hour is spent in tuning the instrument of our souls, repressing idle and unprofitable thoughts, and recollecting the mind from temporal things; and some time, also, is necessary to spend in reaping the fruit of our prayer in the latter end.

Although I cannot deny, but after some pious action, the mind is better disposed for meditation, for as dried wood quickly burneth, so the mind that is well disposed, is sooner kindled with this celestial fire.

The morning also is the best time for meditation, because the mind is then most free from fancies, and therefore can with better facility apply itself to this holy exercise. But who, by reason of the multiplicity of outward affairs, cannot spend so much time? yet, at leastwise, let them, with the poor widow in the gospel, offer up to God the small mite of their sincere affection. And no doubt but he who provideth for all creatures, according to their several necessities, will graciously accept it, if their culpable negligence doth not deserve the contrary.

THE SEVENTH DOCUMENT.

The seventh document is, that he that is visited with divine consolations in or out of prayer, ought to have a special care to spend that time, above other, with fruit unto his soul; for whilst this prosperous gale doth blow, he will go further in his journey towards heaven, in one hour, than otherwise he hath, or shall do, in many days. So did the holy Father, St. Francis do, of whom St. Bonaventure writeth, that he had such a solicitous care of divine visitations, that whensoever upon the way he was recreated with them, he would either go before, or stay behind his companion awhile, until he had digested this divine morsel sent unto him from heaven. They who are negligent and careless to answer divine visitations, are commonly chastised with this punishment from God—that when they seek they will hardly find them.

THE EIGHTH DOCUMENT.

The last document and of greatest moment is, in this exercise of prayer, we must join meditation to contemplation, seeing one is, as it were, a ladder unto the other; wherefore, it is the part of meditation, with diligent attention, to consider and ponderate celestial things, first one, then another, that at last some pious affection may be stirred up in the soul, like him that with a steel striketh fire out of a flint; but it is the property of contemplation, which followeth meditation, to enjoy this kindled fire; that is to say, to embrace that affection, which, with much labor, he hath sought and found, in deep silence and tranquillity of spirit, not with many discourses and speculations of the understanding, but with a pure simple relation, and eye to verity. Hence a certain doctor saith, that meditation doth discourse with labor and small profit, but contemplation without any trouble, and with much fruit; the one doth seek, and the other findeth; the one doth chew, and the other eateth the meat; the one doth reason and consider, the other contemplateth those things she loves and tasteth; and, in fine, the one is the means, the other is the end; the one is the way and motion, the other the term of the way and end of the action. From these things which we have said, that rule or axiom is very frequent amongst spiritual masters, which few of their scholars do rightly understand: that is, *fine adepto media omnia cessare:* the end being attained unto, all means do cease. For example, the mariner resteth when he hath arrived to his desired haven. So he that meditates, when, by the means of meditation, he shall come to the rest and sweet gust of contemplation, ought to leave the cragged way of reasoning and discourse, contenting himself with the memory of Almighty God alone; whom he may behold as present to his soul, and quietly enjoy that sweet affection which he shall vouchsafe to bestow upon him, whether it be of love, admiration, joy, or the like; and the reason is, because the end of this business consisteth rather in love and affection of the will, than in speculations of the understanding. When, therefore, the will hath captivated the one, and attained to the other affection, all reasoning and speculations of the understanding are to be left, that the soul may bend all her forces to it, without a confused wandering to the actions of the other powers. Therefore, a certain doctor giveth this counsel to those who perceive themselves to be inflamed with the fire of divine love; that they should quite abolish all other thoughts and speculations, never so sublime and subtle; not that they are evil, but because, for the present, they hinder a greater good. And this is no other than, after we have come to the end, to leave meditation for the love of contemplation; which we may do (to speak particularly of this matter) in the end of every exercise, (that is to say) after the petition of divine love, as above said, and that for two reasons; first, because it is supposed that the labor of the finished exercise hath produced some fruit of devotion towards Almighty God, as the wise man saith: "*Melius est finis orationis, quam principium*:" "Better is the end of prayer, than the beginning." Secondly, it is expedient that, after labor in prayer, the understanding rest awhile, and recreate itself in the arms of contemplation.

Here let every one resist whatsoever imaginations shall present themselves unto his mind, let him still his understanding, let him fasten his memory strongly upon God; considering that he is placed in his holy presence. But let him not adhere to any particular contemplation of God, but only content himself with that knowledge which faith hath ministered unto him; and to this, let him add his will and affection, seeing this is only that which embraceth God, and in which the whole fruit of meditation consisteth.

The weak understanding is little able to conceive or comprehend anything of God, but the will can love him very much. Let him, therefore, rouse up himself from temporal things, and let him recollect himself within himself, that is to say, to the centre of his soul, where is the lively image of God; here let him hearken attentively, as though he heard Almighty God speaking from a high turret; or as though he held him fast, being present in his soul; or as though there were no other persons in the world, besides God and himself. Nay, I say more, let him quite forget himself, and those things which he doth; for, as one of the ancient holy fathers saith, prayer is then every way complete, when he that prayeth doth not consider that he is before God in prayer, and this is to be done, not only in the end of the exercise, but in the midst, and in every part of meditation. For, as often as this spiritual sleep shall sweetly oppress any one, that is to say, when the understanding is drowned as it were in a sleep, (but the will watching) let him quietly enjoy this delicate meat as long as it shall last. But when it is digested, let him return again to meditation, in which we must behave ourselves like a gardener; who, when he watereth a bed of his garden, after he hath once sprinkled it with water, expecteth awhile, until it be drunk in, then sprinkleth again, that at last it may thoroughly wet the earth, that it may become more fruitful.

But what the soul, cast into this heavenly sleep, and illuminated with the splendor of this eternal light doth enjoy—what satiety! what charity! what internal peace!—no tongue is able to express. This is that peace which exceedeth all understanding; this is that felicity, a greater than which cannot be imagined in this vale of misery.

There are many so inflamed with this fire of divine love, that their interiors, at the very memory of this blessed name, without any meditation at all before, do rest in joy. These need no more consideration or discourses to love God, than a mother needs motives to love her child, or the bride her husband. Others there are so absorbed in God, not only in prayer, but also in outward business, that they wholly forget themselves, and all creatures, for the love of him. Neither are these effects of divine love to be admired, seeing worldly love causeth oftentimes greater matters in the minds of men, that it makes them mad. What! shall we attribute less efficacy to grace than unto nature and sin? When, therefore, the soul shall feel this operation of divine love, in what part of prayer soever it happeneth, let him never refuse it; although he spent all the time of this exercise in it, without any manner of consideration at all, for that point be purposed to meditate upon: (except he be specially obliged unto it) for, as St. Augustine saith, vocal prayer ought to be left, if it hurteth devotion; so, meditation ought to be deferred, if it hurteth contemplation. But as it is necessary to leave meditation for this affection, and to ascend from the lesser to the greater, so, oftentimes, this contemplation is to be left for meditation, when it is so vehement that the corporal health receiveth some damage thereby. This oftentimes happeneth to those who, taken with the pleasure of this divine sweetness, give themselves too indiscretly to these exercises, and use them too immoderately, to whom (as a certain doctor saith,) this will be the best remedy;—that they desist from contemplation, turning their minds to some other good affection; as of compassion in meditating on the sufferings of our Saviour; or about the sins and miseries of this world, to exonerate the heart, diverting it from that too much intension.

THE SECOND PART.

OF

DEVOTION,

AND OF THOSE THINGS WHICH THEREUNTO BELONG.

CHAPTER I.

WHAT IS DEVOTION.

AMONGST all the troublesome difficulties, to which they who frequent the exercises of prayer and meditation, are subject, none is greater, than that which they suffer from the defect of devotion, which often is felt in prayer. For, if they have this, nothing is more sweet, nothing more pleasant, nothing more easy, than to insist to prayer and meditation. But, if that be wanting, nothing more hard, nothing more difficult, nothing more burdensome than to pray. Wherefore, seeing we have already spoken of prayer, meditation, and the method to perform it, now, it will not be beside our

Devotion maketh all things easy.

purpose, to treat of those things which partly promote, and partly hinder and extinguish devotion in the mind of man: as also to lay open the temptations which are obvious to those who frequent these pious exercises; and, last of all, to annex some certain documents, which may not a little avail to the well performance of this business. We will, therefore, begin from the definition of devotion, that it may manifestly appear, what a precious pearl it is for which we war.

Devotion, as St. Thomas saith, is a virtue which maketh a man prompt and ready to every virtuous deed, and stirring him up to do well; which definition evidently showeth, the necessity and utility of this virtue, as containing more in it, than any man can imagine.

For the better understanding of this, we must know, that the chief impediment that hindereth us from leading a virtuous life, is the corruption of human nature, proceeding from sin, which brings with it a vehement inclination to vice, and a great difficulty to do well; this makes the way of virtue cragged and troublesome, although in itself considered, nothing in this world is so sweet, so lovely, so beautiful.

The divine wisdom hath ordained the help of devotion, as a most convenient remedy, to overcome this difficulty; for, as the north wind dissipateth clouds, and maketh a clear sky, so true devotion expelleth, from the mind, the tediousness of this way, and maketh us with alacrity prompt to pious actions. This virtue doth so far forth obtain the name of virtue, that likewise it is a special gift of the Holy Ghost: a heavenly dew, an assistance obtained by prayer, whose property is to remove all difficulties happening in prayer and meditation; to expel tepidity, to minister alacrity in the divine service, to instruct the understanding, to roborate the will, to kindle in our hearts heavenly love, to extinguish the flames of unlawful desires, to engender a hatred and loathing of sin, and all transitory things; and, last of all, to him that possesseth it, to infuse a new fervor, a new spirit, a new mind, and new desires to do well. For, as Samson, as long as he had his hair, did exceed all men in strength, but when that was cut, he was as weak as others; so the soul of every Christian, recreated with the help of devotion, is strong and valiant. But when it is deprived of it, it becometh infirm and weak.

But, above all the praises which can be heaped upon this virtue, this is the chief, that although it be but one only virtue, yet it is a prick and motive to all. They, therefore, that desire to walk in a virtuous way, must get this for a spur, for without it, he will never be able to rule his rebellious flesh.

In what devotion consisteth.

Hence, it manifestly appeareth, in what the true essence of devotion doth consist, not in tenderness of heart, or abundance of consolations, wherewith they who meditate are often recreated, except a prompt alacrity of the mind to do well be thereunto adjoined; especially, seeing it sometimes happeneth, the one to be found without the other, Almighty God so disposing for the trial of his servants. Though I cannot deny, but that these consolations do often proceed from devotion and promptitude of the mind to do well, and, on the contrary, the true devotion is not a little augmented by the same consolations and spiritual gusts; and, therefore, the servants of God may lawfully desire and ask them, not for the delight they bring with them, but because they do greatly increase devotion, which maketh us, with alacrity, to apply ourselves to virtuous actions, which the kingly prophet testifieth of himself saying, "*Viam mandatorum tuorum cucurri, cum dilatasti cor meum:*" "I have run the ways of thy commandments when thou hast enlarged my heart," that is, when thou hast recreated me with the sweetness of thy consolations, which are the cause of this my readiness.

Now let us treat of the means, whereby this virtue is to be attained unto, which will bring no small profit with it, for, seeing it is the spur to all other virtues, to set down the means whereby it is to be obtained, is no other thing, than to prescribe the means to get all other virtues.

CHAPTER II.

NINE MEANS OR HELPS WHEREBY THIS VIRTUE OF DEVOTION MAY BE ATTAINED UNTO, WITH THE LEAST DIFFICULTY.

THE things which promote devotion are many, of which we will handle a few.

Continuance of exercise helpeth devotion.

First, it helpeth much devotion, if those exercises be undertaken with a generous resolution, ready to undergo what difficulty soever shall occur, for the obtaining of this precious pearl. For it is certain, that nothing is excellent which is not difficult, of which kind is devotion, especially in beginnings.

Custody of the heart.

Secondly, a diligent custody of the heart from every vain and unprofitable cogitation, from affections, strange love, and turbulent motions, doth much promote devotion. For it is evident, that every one of these, is no little hinderance, seeing this virtue chiefly requireth a quiet heart, free from all inordinate affection, and so well composed as the strings of a well tuned instrument.

Custody of the senses.

Thirdly, custody of the senses, especially the eyes, tongue and ears, seeing by these, the heart is much distracted. For those things which enter in through the eyes and ears, do strain the mind with divers imaginations, and consequently, disturb and trouble the peace and tranquillity of the soul. Wherefore, one not without cause said, that he that meditateth must be deaf, blind, and dumb; for by how much less he wandereth abroad, with greater recollection, will he rejoice at home.

Solitude.

Fourthly, solitude helpeth devotion much, for it doth not only remove the occasions of sin, and take away the causes which chiefly disturb the heart and senses, but it maketh a solitary man, to rouse up himself from temporal things, to be present to himself, and converse incessantly with God. To which, the opportunity of the place doth admonish, which admitteth no other society.

Reading of spiritual books.

Fifthly, the reading of spiritual books, doth not a little nourish devotion, because it administereth matter of consideration, abstracteth the mind from all things created, stirreth up devotion, and causeth that a man doth sooner adhere to the consideration of those things, which in reading, offered him a more pleasant taste, that, that wherewith the heart aboundeth, may oftener occur to his memory.

Continual memory of God.

Sixthly, continual memory of Almighty God, and daily imagination of his sacred presence, that always thou art in his sight, with a frequent use of aspirations, which St. Augustine calleth jaculatory prayers; for these do guard the palace of the mind, conserving devotion in her fervor, that a man is always willing to pious actions, and ready to holy prayer. This document is one of the principal instruments of a spiritual life, and the only remedy for those, who have neither time nor place with opportunity, to insist to long prayer and meditation; and they which do thus bestow their labor to frequent aspirations, will, in a short time, profit much.

Perseverance. Seventhly, perseverance in good exercises, that so times and places be duly observed, especially morning and evening, as fittest times for prayer.

Corporal austerities. Eighthly, corporal abstinence and austerities do much help devotion, fasting from meat, a frugal table, a a hard bed, hair cloth, discipline, and the like. As they originally proceed from devotion of the mind, so they do not a little cherish, conserve, and nourish the root from whence they spring, which is devotion.

Works of mercy. Lastly, works of mercy, are a great spur unto devotion, because they increase the confidence we have to appear before God, and to be presented before his sacred Majesty. They do accompany our prayers; and, finally, they merit that they be sooner heard by God, especially seeing they proceed from a merciful heart.

CHAPTER III.

NINE IMPEDIMENTS TO DEVOTION.

As there be nine things which do promote devotion, so likewise there be nine impediments that do hinder the same.

Venial sins.

The first impediment of devotion is, sins not only mortal, but also venial, for these, although they do not quite abolish charity, yet, at leastwise, they diminish the fervor of it, and consequently make us less apt to devotion. Wherefore, with all diligence they are to be avoided, not only for the evil they bring with them, but also for the good which they hinder.

Remorse of conscience.

Secondly, remorse of conscience proceeding from sins, when it is in extremes, because it doth disquiet the mind, weakeneth the head, and maketh a man unfit for acts of virtue.

Anxiety of heart.

Thirdly, anxiety of heart, and inordinate sadness, for with these, the delight of a good conscience, and spiritual joy of the inward mind, can hardly suit and agree.

Cares of the mind.

Fourthly, too many cares which do disquiet the mind, like the Egyptian prefects, who did oppress the children of Israel with too immoderate labors, nor will ever suffer them to take that spiritual repose, which they should have often had in prayer. Yea, at that time, above others, they disturb the mind, endeavoring to seduce her from her spiritual exercise.

Affairs. Fifthly, a multitude of affairs, which take up our whole time, suffocates the spirit, scarce leaving for a man a moment to employ in Almighty God's service.

Sixthly, delights and pleasures of the senses, *Delights of the senses.* for these make spiritual exercises unsavoury, and a man unworthy to be recreated with heavenly consolations; for, as St. Bernard saith, he is not worthy of the visitations of the Holy Ghost, that seeketh after worldly solace.

Inordinate delight in eating and drinking. Seventhly, inordinate delight in eating and drinking; especially long and sumptuous suppers, which make a man unapt to spiritual exercises. For when the body is oppressed with too much meat, the spirit cannot so freely elevate itself to God.

Eighthly, curiosity of the senses and under- *Curiosity of the senses.* standing; as to see sights and hear new rumors, because these do spend precious time, disturb and overthrow the tranquillity of the mind; distracting it with many impertinences, which can be no small hinderance to devotion.

Lastly, an intermission of our wonted exer-

Intermission of exercises. cises, except when they are not omitted or deferred for a pious cause, or just necessity. For the spirit of devotion is delicate; which, when it is gone, it hardly returneth again, at least with great difficulty. For as trees and plants must be watered in due season, otherwise they wither away and perish, so devotion, except it be watered with the waters of holy meditation, doth easily vanish.

These things we have set down briefly, that they may be the better remembered; use and experience of them will afford a longer explication.

CHAPTER IV.

OF THE COMMON TEMPTATIONS, WHICH FOR THE MOST PART, ASSAULT THOSE WHO GIVE THEMSELVES TO MEDITATION; AS ALSO OF THE REMEDIES AGAINST THEM.

Now, let us see with what temptations, they, who frequent the exercise of prayer and meditation, are molested, that we may provide convenient remedies for them, which be these:—First, the want of spiritual consolations. Second, a multitude of unprofitable thoughts. Third, thoughts of infidelity and blasphemy. Fourth, fancies in the night. Fifth, sleepiness and drowsiness. Sixth, diffidence of going forward. Seventh, too much presumption of their own sanctity. Eighth, inordinate desire of learning. Ninth, indiscreet zeal.

These are the common temptations which do trouble those, who lead a virtuous life.

A REMEDY FOR THE FIRST TEMPTATION.

What to do in the time of dryness of spirit.

To him that wanteth spiritual consolations, this is the remedy, that, therefore, he omitteth not his customary exercises of prayer, although they seem unsavory, and of no fruit;

but let him set himself in the presence of God, coming before him, as guilty of many grievous sins; let him search, diligently, the corners of his own conscience, and consider whether or no through his own default, he hath lost this grace, if so, let him beseech Almighty God to pardon him for this sin, admiring the inestimable riches of his divine patience in tolerating us so long.

By this means he will reap no small fruit from his aridity of spirit, taking from thence, occasion of profounder humility, when he considereth his own malice and perverseness in heaping up of sin, or of more ardent affection, when he seeth Almighty God's goodness in pardoning the same. And, although he enjoyeth no pleasure at all in his exercises, let him not, therefore, abstain from the continuation of them, for it is not always necessary that it should be sweet and savoury to the present taste, which will be hereafter profitable. Especially when it is often seen by experience, that those who constantly persevere in their intended exercises, not giving over in the time of this aridity, but continue them with what care and diligence possibly they are able, that these I say, depart from this table recreated with many heavenly consolations, and much spiritual joy, seeing they find nothing to be omitted on their parts. It

The reward of those who in the time of dryness of spirit, do not leave off their wonted exercise.

is but a small matter to protract prayer for a long space when it floweth with consolations, but when these are taken away, not to desist, is an admirable act of virtue; for in this humility shineth, patience is eminent, and true perseverance in good works is manifested.

But it is necessary in the time of aridity, to have a greater care of himself, watching over himself with greater diligence, to discuss his conscience more sincerely, and to observe all his words and actions more accurately. For then, when alacrity and spiritual joy (which is the principal oar of his navigation) is absent, with greater vigilance the defect of grace is to be supplied.

When thou findest thyself to be in this state, thou oughtest to think, as St. Bernard admonisheth, that the sentinels which did watch thee, are asleep, that the walls that did defend thee, are broken down, and therefore, the only hope of safeguard to consist in arms, when all is gone which did otherwise protect thee, safety is to be sought with an armed hand. O what deserved glory followeth such a soul, which winneth the triumphant laurel after such a manner, she fighteth a combat with the enemy, without either sword or buckler, is valiant without help, who, although she be alone, sustaineth the whole battle, with as much courage, as though she were compassed round about with troops of auxiliary forces.

This is the chiefest proof, whereby the sincerity and goodness of the friends of God is known, whereby the true are severed from false servants.

A REMEDY FOR THE SECOND TEMPTATION.

What to do when we have unprofitable thoughts.

Against the temptation of importune and unprofitable cogitations, which are wont to vex those that pray, and disquiet them with no small molestation, this is the remedy; to resist them manfully, provided always, the resistance be not joined with too much violence and anxiety of spirit. Seeing this work dependeth not so much of our strength, as Almighty God's grace and profound humility; wherefore, when any one is beset with these temptations, let him confidently turn himself to God without any scruple or anxiety of mind, (seeing this is no fault, or at least, a very small one,) with great submission and devotion of heart, saying, behold, Lord, behold what I am! what other thing can be looked for from this ordure, but such filthy savours? what other fruit can be expected from this earth, which thou didst curse in the beginning of the world, but thorns and thistles? what good can it bring forth, except thou, Lord, dost purge it from all corruption? this being said, let him return to continue his meditations with patience, expecting the visitation of our Lord, who is never wanting to the humble of spirit.

If yet the tumult of these troublesome fancies doth not cease, nevertheless, let him still resist constantly, repelling the force of them to the utmost of his power. From this perseverant battle, believe me, he will reap more gain and merit, than if; he had enjoyed the greatest consolations in his meditation.

A REMEDY FOR THE THIRD TEMPTATION.

Temptation of thoughts of blasphemy, ought to be contemned.

To overcome the temptation of blasphemous thoughts, we must know as there is no temptation so troublesome to a pious mind, so likewise, there is none less dangerous; therefore, the best remedy is to contemn them, for seeing sin consisteth not in sense, but delight of those things we think of. But in these there is no pleasure, but rather torture; therefore, they may challenge the name of punishment rather than of sin; and the more vexation is in them, the further off we are from consenting unto any sin; therefore it is best not to fear, but contemn them, seeing fear maketh them more strong and violent.

A REMEDY FOR THE FOURTH TEMPTATION.

Against the temptations of infidelity, he who is vexed with such cogitations on the one side, let him consider the imbecility of man's condition on the other side, the greatness of the divine power, to whom nothing is impossible; those things which God hath commanded, let him always bear in mind; for others, let him never busy himself in searching curiously the works of Supreme Majesty, seeing the least of them do so far transcend human capacity. Wherefore, he that desireth to enter into this sanctuary of God's works, let him enter with profound humility and reverence, endued with the eyes of a simple dove, not of a subtile serpent; and let him bear the mind of a meek disciple, and not of a temerarious judge; let him put on the shape of a child, for such our Lord maketh partakers of his divine secrets; let him not mind to search or know the causes of God's works; let him shut the eyes of natural reason, and open the eyes of faith: for these are the hands wherewith God's works ought to be handled. Human understanding is able to comprehend the works of men, but not of God, seeing they are not capable of so much light.

In considering God's works good heed ought to be taken.

This temptation, seeing it is one of the greatest, which doth assault men, and bringeth none, or small delight with it, is to be cured with the remedy of the precedent temptation; that is, to make slight of it, for it cannot stain the soul with any great blemish, because where the will is contrary, there is no danger of any sin.

A REMEDY FOR THE FIFTH TEMPTATION.

THERE are some who are troubled with many fears and fancies when they go to pray in solitary places, remote from the company of men, against which temptation, there is no more efficacious remedy, than for a man to arm himself with a courageous mind, persevering in his exercise, for this fear is overcome with fighting, not with flying; moreover, let him consider, that the devil, nor any other thing whatsoever can hurt us, except God permits Let him also consider, that we are compassed about with a custody of angels, which do guard us, as well in, as out of prayer; they assist us carrying up our prayers to heaven; they help us to bring to nothing the devices of our crafty enemy, and to confound all his mischievous plots.

Fear overcome with fighting not with flying.

A REMEDY FOR THE SIXTH TEMPTATION.

Drowsiness in prayer ariseth from a three-fold cause.

To overcome sleep, wherewith some that meditate are often molested, we must consider that sometimes it proceedeth from mere necessity, and then it is not to be denied the body what is its due, lest it hindereth what is our right. Sometimes it proceedeth out of infirmity; then he must take heed not to vex himself too much, seeing herein is no sin at all, but moderately, as much as strength suffereth, resisting it; now using some industry, then some small violence, that prayer doth not altogether perish, without which nothing in this life can be had secure: but when it cometh out of sloth, or from the devil, then there is no better remedy than to abstain from wine, and not to use water in abundance, but as much as quencheth his thirst; to pray upon his knees, or after some other painful gesture of the body, let him use discipline, or other corporal austerity, to drive sleep from his eyes. To conclude, the remedy for this and all others, is instantly to implore his assistance, who is ready to give it to all, so they ask it fervently and constantly.

A REMEDY FOR THE SEVENTH TEMPTATION.

Man ought chiefly to rely upon God's grace not his own merits.

Against the temptations of diffidence and presumption, seeing that they in themselves be contrary, it is requisite to apply divers remedies. Against diffidence, let him consider that we do not rest upon our own merits, but upon Almighty God's grace; who is so much the more willing to assist man, by how much the more he is diffident of his own forces, placing a firm hope in the goodness of God, to whom nothing is impossible: the remedy for presumption, is to consider that the most evident and certain argument is, that a man is yet furthest from true sanctity, when he thinketh himself to be nearest.

Moreover, let him look upon himself in the lives of the saints who now reign with Christ, or live yet in this mortal life, as in a looking-glass, to which of these he doth compare himself, he will see that he is no more than a dwarf in respect of a giant; which consideration will not a little suppress his pride.

A REMEDY FOR THE EIGHTH TEMPTATION.

The divine wisdom doth infinitely exceed human prudence.

AGAINST the inordinate desire of study and learning, it is good to consider how far virtue exceedeth science, and how much the knowledge of God excelleth human wisdom. Hence a man may learn how necessary it is, to bestow more labor upon one, than upon the other. Moreover, the world hath all the excellence that can be desired, but cannot avoid this misery—that it must end with life. What, then, more miserable than to seek after that, with so much labor and expense, which so quickly perisheth? If all things in the world could be known, they are but as nothing; and, therefore, it is much better to exercise ourselves in the love of God, the fruit whereof remaineth for ever, and in whom we see and know all things. Last of all, in the day of judgment we shall not be asked what we have read, but what we have done; not how eloquently we have spoken, but how well we have lived.

A REMEDY FOR THE NINTH TEMPTATION.

The salvation of our neighbor is so to be regarded that we do not neglect our own selves.

THE chiefest remedy against indiscreet zeal of helping others, is so to attend to the good of our neighbors, that we hurt not ourselves: and so to have a care of the consciences of others, that we neglect not our own; but in assisting them, it is good to reserve so much time as is sufficient to conserve the heart in devotion and recollection. And this is, as St. Paul saith: "*Ambulare in spiritu:*" "To walk in spirit;" that is to say, that a man be more in God than in himself. Seeing, therefore, that the prime root of all our good upon this dependeth, we must strive that our prayer be so profound and long as may conserve the soul in devotion, which every short meditation is not able to do, but devout and long meditation.

CHAPTER V.

OTHER CERTAIN ADMONITIONS NECESSARY FOR SPIRITUAL PERSONS.

The thing that affordeth greatest difficulty in this spiritual journey is, to know how to come to God, and to converse with him familiarly. Let, therefore, none dare to enter in this way without a good guide, and well instructed with necessary admonitions and documents, of which we will set down a few, according to our wonted brevity.

The first is whereby we are taught what end we must aim at in these our spiritual exercises. We must therefore know, that since to communicate with Almighty God of itself is most delightful, having no bitterness mixed with it, as the wise man testifieth: hence it cometh to pass that many, allured with the pleasure of this admirable and unused sweetness, (which is greater than can be comprehended) come to God, and frequent these spiritual actions; as reading, prayer, meditation, use of the Sacrament, for the great content and delight they take in them, so that for the principal end, wherewith they are moved, is this admirable sweetness which they vehemently de-

The error and abuse of some.

sire. This is a great error, and many are plunged into it; for seeing to love and seek God should be the chiefest end of all our actions, these love and seek themselves; that is to say, their own gust and sensible delight rather than God, which was the scope of the contemplative philosophy of the gentiles; especially as a certain doctor saith, that this is a kind of avarice, luxury, and spiritual gluttony, no less pernicious than carnal. From this error springeth another branch; to wit, that many judge themselves and others, according to the ebbing and flowing of consolations, so far that they are persuaded that a man is more or less perfect, by how much more or less he is visited with divine consolations. This is a great mistake.

What should be the end of spiritual exercises.

Against both these temptations, this general doctrine is a remedy: that every one must know that the scope of all these exercises, and the chief end of a spiritual life, is the observing of God's commandments, and a perfect fulfilling of his divine will: to this it is necessary that our own will be mortified, that the will of God may the better live and reign in us; seeing both these are directly contrary the one to the other. But this noble victory, seeing it cannot be obtained without special favor and allurements of God, therefore we ought to frequent the exercise of prayer, the better by it (and indeed the only means) to obtain this grace, and to bring this serious business of our soul's perfection to a good and desired end. With this intention we may confidently desire of God internal consolation, as we have said before. This did the prophet David, when he said: "*Redde mihi Domini lætitiam salutaris tui, et spiritu principali confirma me:*" "Give me, O Lord, the joy of thy salvation, and confirm me with thy principal spirit."

Hence it is manifest what end every one ought to prefix to himself in these exercises, and how they should esteem and measure their own and other's profit; not according to the multitude of flowing consolations, but according to those things they have constantly suffered for God, partly in fulfilling his divine pleasure, partly in renouncing their own proper wills.

And that this ought to be the end of all our prayer and reading, it appeareth by that one psalm of the prophet David which beginneth "*Beati immaculati in via, qui ambulant in lege Domini:*" "Blessed are the immaculate in the way, which walk in the law of the Lord;" which is the longest psalm in the psalter, notwithstanding, there is not one verse in it, in which there is not mention of the law of God, and keeping his commandments: which the Holy Ghost hath so ordained, that men may learn to direct all prayer and reading to this end and scope. From which they that do decline, cast themselves into the secret snares of the enemy, who with his subtle craft persuadeth them, that is, some great matter which, indeed, is nothing; and for this cause men, most exercised in spiritual matters, do affirm the only touchstone of true virtue to be, not that sensible delight which is found in prayer, but patience in affliction, abnegation of one's own self, a sincere and entire fulfilling of the divine will, and, finally, in a diligent observing of Almighty God's laws and commandments; though I must confess that prayer itself, and the frequent consolations that are found therein, do not a little conduce and help to the better effecting of these things before mentioned.

They who are desirous to know how much progress they have made in the way of God, let them examine how much they have increased in interior and exterior humility; how willingly they have put up with injuries; with what mind they have borne with others' infirmities; how they have compassionated the imperfections of their neighbors; what confidence they have had in God, in the tedious time of tribulation; how they have bridled their tongues; how they have kept their heart; how they have mortified their flesh, and made it subject to the spirit: with what moderation they have behaved themselves in prosperity and adversity; with what gravity and discretion they have governed all their actions: and, above all, how dead they have been to the world, with all its pleasures, honors, and dignities; and accordingly as they have profited in these virtues, let them measure their perfection, and not according to the consolations wherewith God hath visited them. Wherefore, let every one be sure to bear one hand,

and the chiefest over himself in mortification, the other in prayer, seeing the one cannot be attained unto without the other.

THE SECOND ADMONITION.

As it is not lawful to desire consolations and spiritual comforts, to that end that in them we should set up our rest, but only as they assist us in our spiritual progress, much less is it lawful to wish for visions, revelations, and the like; which to those who are not well grounded in humility, may be a great cause of their utter ruin. Neither is there any reason to fear that those who refuse or reject them, should be disobedient to God; because when it shall please God to reveal anything, he will do it after such a fashion that he to whom such things shall be revealed shall be so certain of them, that he will have no reason either to fear or doubt, though he should himself never so much strive against them.

THE THIRD ADMONITION.

We must have a special care not to speak to others of those sensible consolations, which Almighty God hath been pleased to recreate us withal: except it be to our spiritual director. Hence it is, that that mellifluous Doctor was wont to advise every one to have these words written in great letters in his chamber: My secret to myself: my secret to myself.

THE FOURTH MEDITATION.

Moreover we must always take good heed to deal with God, with much humility and reverence, never to esteem ourselves so high in his favor, as to neglect to cast down our eyes upon our own baseness, and to shrowd our wings in the presence of so great a majesty, as holy Augustine was wont to do, of whom it is written, that he had learned to rejoice before God with fear and trembling.

THE FIFTH ADMONITION.

We have heretofore counselled the servant of God, that he consecrateth some certain time of the day to recollection. But now besides the ordinary course, we say, that he must sometimes sequester himself from all business and employments, as much as is possible, and give himself wholly over to devotion, the better to nourish his soul with the abundance of spiritual dainties, recovering his daily losses, and getting new force to go forward in his spiritual journey. Which, although it be not amiss to do at all times, yet more specially, upon the principal feasts of the year, in the time of temptation ; after a long journey ; after troublesome business, which gave matter of much distraction, that when we exclude from our souls all exterior things, and call ourselves back again to the point from whence we did digress.

THE SIXTH ADMONITION.

There be many who be not discreet in their spiritual exercises, when they enjoy heavenly consolations, and it oftentimes falleth out, that this prosperity doth expose them to manifest peril, for when Almighty God showereth down more abundantly this celestial dew upon their souls, they are so ravished with the sweetness of it, that they addict themselves without measure to this only exercise; to this end they prolong the time of prayer, macerate themselves with watching and other corporal austerities, so that nature itself, at length, is constrained to sink under the burthen of such indiscreet mortification. Hence it cometh to pass, that many abhor spiritual exercises, and some are not only made by this means unfit for corporal, but also dull for spiritual labors of prayer and meditation. Wherefore, in all these, there is great need of discretion, especially in the beginning, when spiritual consolations be more fervent, and commonly when discretion is least: for we must so order our diet that we do not faint in the midst of our journey. On the contrary, there be some so slothful and undevout, that under the color of discretion, immoderately make much of themselves, refusing the least labor or trouble. This, although, it be dangerous to all, but especially to beginners; for as St. Bernard saith, it is impossible that he should persevere long in a spiritual course, who is indiscreet at first. That when he is a novice esteemeth himself wise, and when he is young governeth himself like an old man. Neither can I easily judge which of these be more dangerous: except as Thomas a Kempis saith, the first is more incurable, for whilst the body is strong and sound, there may be hopes to cure tepidity; but when it is once weakened through indiscretion, it scarce ever can be brought to its former fervor.

THE SEVENTH ADMONITION.

THERE is yet another danger more pernicious than the former, which is, that some having experience of this inestimable virtue of prayer, that all the fruit of a spiritual life doth depend upon it. Hence they persuade themselves, that in it all is contained, and that only, that virtue doth suffice for our salvation, which makes them to neglect other virtues, which are likewise the foundations and props which do uphold a spiritual building, which being taken away the whole fabric falleth to ruin; wherefore, they that seek after this one only virtue, with such indiscreet avidity, the more they labor the less fruit they reap. But the servant of God that expecteth merit and comfort in the way of perfection, must not fix his eyes so much upon one only virtue, although it be never so rare and excellent, but generally attend to all, as one string upon an instrument maketh no music, except we strike the rest, so one virtue cannot make a spiritual harmony in our souls, if the other be wanting, not unlike a clock, which if there be but a fault in one wheel, the others will stand; so it is in a spiritual clock, if one virtue be deficient.

THE EIGHTH ADMONITION.

THESE things which we have hitherto said, which do help to devotion, are so to be taken himself to Almighty God's grace, and behave himself manfully in his holy service, with this caution, that we should not put our confidence in them, but in God.

This I say, because there are some who labor to reduce all rules into art, thinking that they have attained to the perfection of that exercise, if they observe exactly the rules thereof. But they who put good principles into practice, will quickly attain unto their desired end, which doing, they are not to reduce grace into art, nor to attribute that to human rules, which is the gift of God. Hence we say, that it is not necessary to follow these rules, and documents, as depending of art, but as instruments of grace; because a man will learn thus to know, that the principal means, which one ought to seek after, is profound humility, with the consideration of our own baseness, and a great confidence in Almighty God's mercy. To the end, that we may come to the knowledge of the one and the other, let us pour out tears without intermission, and continually pray, that as we expect at the gate of humility, so we may obtain by it all our desires, and persevere in humble thanksgiving to the divine bounty, without any trust to our own works, or to any thing that is ours.

AD HONOREM DEI.